BARRON'S BOOK NOTES

Y0-DOM-381

Beowulf

BY

Lewis Warsh

SERIES EDITOR

Michael Spring
Editor, *Literary Cavalcade*
Scholastic Inc.

BARRON'S

BARRON'S EDUCATIONAL SERIES, INC.
Woodbury, New York / London / Toronto / Sydney

ACKNOWLEDGMENTS

We would like to acknowledge the many painstaking hours of work Holly Hughes and Thomas F. Hirsch have devoted to making the *Book Notes* series a success.

All inquiries should be addressed to:
Barron's Educational Series, Inc.
113 Crossways Park Drive
Woodbury, New York 11797

Library of Congress Catalog Card No. 84-18416

International Standard Book No. 0-8120-3403-1

Library of Congress Cataloging in Publication Data
Warsh, Lewis.
  Beowulf.

  (Barron's book notes)
  Bibliography: p. 91
  Summary: A guide to reading "Beowulf" with a critical
and appreciative mind. Includes background on the
author's life and times, sample tests, term paper
suggestions, and a reading list.
  1. Beowulf. [1. Beowulf. 2. English literature—
History and criticism] I. Title. I. Series.
PR1585.W34   1984   829'.3   84-18416
ISBN 0-8120-3403-1

PRINTED IN THE UNITED STATES OF AMERICA

456   550   98765432

CONTENTS

ADVISORY BOARD

We wish to thank the following educators who helped us focus our *Book Notes* series to meet student needs and critiqued our manuscripts to provide quality materials.

HOW TO USE THIS BOOK

You have to know how to approach literature in order to get the most out of it. This *Barron's Book Notes* volume follows a plan based on methods used by some of the best students to read a work of literature.

Begin with the guide's section on the author's life and times. As you read, try to form a clear picture of the author's personality, circumstances, and motives for writing the work. This background usually will make it easier for you to hear the author's tone of voice, and follow where the author is heading.

Then go over the rest of the introductory material—such sections as those on the plot, characters, setting, themes, and style of the work. Underline, or write down in your notebook, particular things to watch for, such as contrasts between characters and repeated literary devices. At this point, you may want to develop a system of symbols to use in marking your text as you read. (Of course, you should only mark up a book you own, not one that belongs to another person or a school.) Perhaps you will want to use a different letter for each character's name, a different number for each major theme of the book, a different color for each important symbol or literary device. Be prepared to mark up the pages of your book as you read. Put your marks in the margins so you can find them again easily.

Now comes the moment you've been waiting for—the time to start reading the work of literature. You may want to put aside your *Barron's Book Notes* volume until you've read the work all the way through. Or you may want to alternate, reading the *Book Notes* analysis of each section as soon as you have finished reading the corresponding part of the original. Before you move on, reread crucial passages you don't fully understand. (Don't take this guide's analysis for granted—make up your own mind as to what the work means.)

Once you've finished the whole work of literature, you may want to review it right away, so you can firm up your ideas about what it means. You may want to leaf through the book concentrating on passages you marked in reference to one character or one theme. This is also a good time to reread the *Book Notes* introductory material, which pulls together insights on specific topics.

When it comes time to prepare for a test or to write a paper, you'll already have formed ideas about the work. You'll be able to go back through it, refreshing your memory as to the author's exact words and perspective, so that you can support your opinions with evidence drawn straight from the work. Patterns will emerge, and ideas will fall into place; your essay question or term paper will almost write itself. Give yourself a dry run with one of the sample tests in the guide. These tests present both multiple-choice and essay questions. An accompanying section gives answers to the multiple-choice questions as well as suggestions for writing the essays. If you have to select a term paper topic, you may choose one from the list of suggestions in this book. This guide also provides you with a reading list, to help you when you start research for a term paper, and a selection of provocative comments by critics, to spark your thinking before you write.

THE AUTHOR
AND HIS TIMES

Who wrote *Beowulf*—the oldest known epic poem written in English—is a question that has mystified readers for centuries. It's generally thought that the poem was performed orally by the poet before a "live" audience, and that in this way it eventually passed down to readers and listeners. Another theory is that the poem was recited by memory by a "scop," a traveling entertainer who went from court to court, singing songs and telling stories, until it was finally written down at the request of a king who wanted to hear it again.

Because there are three major battle scenes in the poem, some readers believe that *Beowulf* was composed by three different authors. Other readers claim that the sections that take place in Denmark and the sections that occur after Beowulf returns to Geatland were the work of different authors. The majority of critics agree that because of the unified structure of the poem, with its interweaving of historical information into the flow of the main narrative, the poem was most likely composed by one person.

As you read the poem try to imagine yourself in the banquet hall of a large castle, eating and drinking with your friends. The court entertainer—much like a stand-up comedian in a nightclub—begins telling his story. Your presence in the hall means that you're probably a member of the aristocratic class, either a descendant of the founder of a particular tribe or one of your king's followers. (Anglo-Saxon society was divided into two main classes: the aristocracy and the proletariat. *Beowulf*, as you'll see, gives us very little information about the life of the average person in Anglo-Saxon society, but concerns itself exclusively with life in the court and on the battlefield.)

Most of the stories were written and recited during this time to entertain and instruct the members of the aristocratic class. The scop assumed that his audience was familiar with the stories of ancient times. It was his job to make them as interesting and as vivid as possible.

THE POEM

The Plot

Beowulf begins with a history of the Danish kings, starting with Shild (whose funeral is described in the Prologue) and leading up to the reign of King Hrothgar, Shild's great-grandson. Hrothgar is well loved by his people and successful in war. He builds a lavish hall, called Herot, to house his vast army, and when the hall is finished the Danish soldiers gather under its roof to celebrate.

Grendel, a monster in human shape who lives at the bottom of a nearby swamp, is provoked by the singing and carousing of Hrothgar's followers. He appears at the hall late one night and kills thirty of the warriors in their sleep. For the next twelve years the fear of Grendel's potential fury casts a shadow over the lives of the Danes. Hrothgar and his advisers can think of nothing to appease the monster's anger.

Beowulf, prince of the Geats, hears about Hrothgar's troubles, gathers fourteen of the bravest Geat warriors, and sets sail from his home in southern Sweden. The Geats are greeted by the members of Hrothgar's court, and Beowulf boasts to the king of his previous successes as a warrior, particularly his success in fighting sea monsters. Hrothgar welcomes the arrival of the Geats, hoping that Beowulf will live up to his reputation. During the banquet that follows Beowulf's arrival, Unferth, a Danish soldier, voices doubt about Beowulf's past accomplishments, and Beowulf, in turn, accuses Unferth of killing his brothers. Before retiring for the night, Hrothgar promises Beowulf great treasures if he meets with success against the monster.

Grendel appears on the night of the Geats' arrival at Herot. Beowulf, true to his word, wrestles the monster barehanded. He tears off the monster's arm at the shoulder, but Grendel escapes, only to die soon afterward at the bottom of his snake-infested swamp. The Danish warriors, who had fled the hall in fear, return singing songs in praise of Beowulf's triumph. The heroic stories of Siegmund and Hermod, and of the Frisian king Finn, are performed in Beowulf's honor. Hrothgar rewards Beowulf with a great store of treasures. After another banquet the warriors of both the Geats and the Danes retire for the night.

Unknown to the warriors, however, Grendel's mother is plotting revenge. She arrives at the hall when all the warriors are sleeping and carries off Esher, Hrothgar's chief adviser. Beowulf, rising to the occasion, offers to dive to the bottom of the lake, find the monster's dwelling place, and destroy her. He and his men follow the monster's tracks to the cliff overlooking the lake where Grendel's mother lives. They see Esher's bloody head floating on the surface of the lake. While preparing for battle, Beowulf asks Hrothgar to protect his warriors, and to send his treasures to his uncle, King Higlac, if he doesn't return safely.

During the ensuing battle Grendel's mother carries Beowulf to her underwater home. After a terrible fight Beowulf kills the monster with a magical sword that he finds on the wall of her home. He also finds Grendel's dead body, cuts off the head, and returns to land, where the Geat and Danish warriors are waiting expectantly. Beowulf has now purged Denmark of the race of evil monsters.

The warriors return to Hrothgar's court, where the Danish king delivers a sermon to Beowulf on the dangers of pride and on the fleeting nature of fame and power. The Danes and Geats prepare a feast in celebration of the death of the monsters. In the morning the Geats hurry to their boat, anxious to begin the trip home. Beowulf bids farewell to Hrothgar and tells the old king that if the Danes ever again need help he will gladly come to their assistance. Hrothgar presents Beowulf with more treasures and they embrace, emotionally, like father and son.

The Geats sail home. After recounting the story of his battles with Grendel and Grendel's mother, Beowulf tells King Higlac about the feud between Denmark and their enemies, the Hathobards. He describes the proposed peace settlement, in which Hrothgar will give his daughter Freaw to Ingeld, king of the Hathobards, but predicts that the peace will not last long. Higlac rewards Beowulf for his bravery with parcels of land, swords, and houses.

The meeting between Higlac and Beowulf marks the end of the first part of the poem. In the next part Higlac is dead, and Beowulf has been king of the Geats for fifty years. A thief steals a jeweled cup from a sleeping dragon who avenges his loss by flying through the night burning down houses, including Beowulf's own hall and throne. Beowulf goes to the cave where the dragon lives, vowing to destroy it single-handed. He's an old man now, however, and his strength is not as great as it was when he fought against Grendel. During the battle Beowulf breaks his sword against the dragon's side; the dragon, enraged, engulfs Beowulf in flames and wounds him in the neck. All of Beowulf's followers flee except Wiglaf, who rushes through the flames to assist the aging warrior. Wiglaf stabs the dragon with his sword, and Beowulf, in a final act of courage, cuts the dragon in half with his knife.

Yet the damage is done. Beowulf realizes that he's dying, that he has fought his last battle. He asks Wiglaf to bring him the dragon's storehouse of treasures; seeing the jewels and gold will make him feel that the effort has been worthwhile. He instructs Wiglaf to build a tomb to be known as "Beowulf's tower" on the edge of the sea. After Beowulf dies, Wiglaf admonishes the troops who deserted their leader when he was fighting against the dragon. He tells them that they have been untrue to the standards of bravery, courage, and loyalty that Beowulf has taught.

Wiglaf sends a messenger to a nearby encampment of Geat soldiers with instructions to report the outcome of the battle. The messenger predicts that the enemies of the Geats will feel free to attack them now that their king is dead. Wiglaf supervises the building of the funeral pyre. In keeping with Beowulf's instructions, the dragon's treasure is buried alongside Beowulf's ashes in the tomb. The poem ends as it began—with the funeral of a great warrior.

NOTE: *Beowulf* is written in an early form of English called Old English, or Anglo-Saxon. The *Beowulf* you read today is a translation from Anglo-Saxon into modern English. If the translation you have shows different spellings of characters' names from what appears here, do not be alarmed. It is the translator's choice to interpret the Anglo-Saxon in a particular

way, and thus minor differences do occur. To avoid
any possible confusion, read the glossary near the end
of this study guide.

Line references and spellings in this guide are based
on the popular Burton Raffel translation (New American Library).

The Characters

Beowulf

A hero must be judged by the things he does and the way he reacts and relates to other people. His deeds must be marked by a nobility of purpose, and he must be willing to risk his life for his ideals. Though Beowulf obviously meets these requirements, he's also a mortal human being. To understand Beowulf it's important to understand how the poet attempts to reconcile the "human" and the "heroic" sides of his personality.

The poet first describes Beowulf as ". . . greater/And stronger than anyone anywhere in this world" (195), without informing us about what he did to acquire this reputation. We see him initially through the awestruck eyes of the Danish soldier patrolling the cliffs. "Nor have I ever seen/," the soldier says, addressing the Geats, "Out of all the men on earth, one greater/Than has come with you" (247-49). Beowulf's appearance—his size, his armor—obviously commands immediate respect and attention.

We learn about his character from the speeches he makes to the soldier and to Wulfgar, the Danish warrior who again asks the Geats to identify themselves. Beowulf—anxious to meet with Hrothgar, from whom he hopes to receive permission to battle Grendel—is courteous, patient, and diplomatic. His manner lacks the brusqueness and coldness of a person whose previous accomplishments make him feel superior to other people. His fame as the world's bravest person hasn't gone to his head.

Yet he's also a person with a definite purpose. If he expects to battle Grendel, he must convince Hrothgar of his bravery. Some of you might find his boastfulness disturbing—as Unferth does—but for Beowulf it's simply a means of getting what he wants.

The question remains, however: What *does* Beowulf want? Is he motivated to perform heroic acts simply by a need to help other people? Are fame and glory uppermost in his mind? Or is he interested mainly in accumulating as much wealth as possible?

It might be best to assume that Beowulf is motivated by a combination of all these things. A hero, the poet is telling us, isn't immune from inner conflicts. He may act selflessly, governed by a code of ethics and an intuitive understanding of other people. But part of him—and this is perhaps the tragic flaw in Beowulf's character—has no real idea of *why* he acts the way he does.

His capacity for forgiveness and generosity is most evident in his relationship with Unferth. When the Danish warrior jealously attempts to slander Beowulf's reputation, Beowulf accuses him of cowardice for not having killed Grendel himself. Beowulf feels that it's important to defend himself, to set the record straight, but he isn't interested in holding grudges. When Unferth later offers him his special sword to fight Grendel's mother, Beowulf accepts, forgivingly, as if the initial encounter had never happened.

Some of you will want to interpret Beowulf's heroic nature as a kind of inner quest, a search for something beyond the ordinary run of existence. Part of this quest involves the search for a true father. In his desire to impress Hrothgar and Higlac, he acts very much the way a son might act toward his father. One of the reasons he comes to help Hrothgar, we learn, is to pay his father's debt. He has no great desire to become king of the Geats. When first offered the throne, he refuses, preferring to play the role of warrior-son. (The father-son relationship runs parallel to the relationship between king and warrior, where a warrior has a duty to serve his king.)

Beowulf's spiritual conflicts—whether to act self-lessly for the good of others, or to accumulate rewards and personal fame—are also a key to his personality. In the same sense, he's never certain whether his success as a warrior is due to his own strength or to God's help. The conflict between the material and the spiritual is never more evident than in his dying words: " 'For this, this gold, these jewels, I thank/Our Father in Heaven, Ruler of the Earth' " (2794–95). Whether Beowulf's inability to resolve this conflict makes him any less worthy of being called a hero is for you to decide.

Hrothgar

Hrothgar is the most human character in the poem, and the person with whom we can most easily identify. He isn't afraid to hide his emotions in a society where it is a sign of weakness for a man to show his feelings, and this characteristic gives him a heroic quality of his own.

When we first meet him he's coming to the end of his reign over the Danish kingdom. To commemorate his various successes he builds a huge hall, Herot, to house his warriors. He's under the illusion that this hall will be a permanent monument to his achievements, something that will exist long after he's dead. This modest show of vanity is Hrothgar's only flaw, and in a way the entire poem revolves around the building of the great hall. (It's as if any display of pride or vanity brings out the evil in the world; if Herot hadn't been built, Grendel might never have attacked the Danish people.) His world outlook is typical of most of the people in Anglo-Saxon society, but less extreme; the poet makes no mention of treachery or conspiracy in Hrothgar's past. Though the world exists in a constant state of flux, everyone desires a feeling of permanence and security. Hrothgar, by building Herot, wants to deny the transitoriness of life. The first part of the poem—dominated by Beowulf's battles with Grendel and Grendel's mother—illustrates the impossibility of his dream.

The virtues of a good warrior are wisdom and courage. A good king, however, must possess not only these qualities, but he also must be concerned for the welfare of his people. Hrothgar possesses wisdom, but his courage—when we meet him he is, after all, an old man—is lacking. When Grendel attacks the hall, all Hrothgar can do is hold his head in despair. Lacking the strength of his youth, he can no longer make decisions in situations involving violence.

After Grendel's mother attacks the hall—and escapes with the body of Esher, Hrothgar's closest friend—we see Hrothgar trembling "in anger and grief" (1308). When Beowulf comes to find out what's wrong, Hrothgar practically begs him to kill the monster. His grief, at this point, verges on hysteria. But given the same circumstances, who wouldn't feel the same? If age robs you of the power to act decisively, it also puts you in touch with your emotions. Hrothgar is wise enough to realize that he isn't strong enough to battle the monster alone. (In this sense, he's unlike Beowulf, who, as an aging king, attempts to relive his youth by fighting the dragon.)

Hrothgar's strongest moment occurs after the battle between Beowulf and Grendel's mother. He delivers a sermon to Beowulf on the evils of pride, advising Beowulf to guard against wickedness and to use his powers for the betterment of other people. He cites the example of Hermod, a king who might have performed great acts of courage, but who instead abused his potential and brought only destruction and slaughter to his people. He warns Beowulf against thinking that just because he's defeated Grendel and Grendel's mother, he has rid the world of evil forever. Death will come to everyone, even those blessed by God. Before you know it, all your strength and power are gone.

Hrothgar's understanding of human nature is based on his long experience as the king of the Danes. He isn't jealous of Beowulf's strength and fame; all he wants is to die knowing he did his best to protect his people from the evils of the world.

Hrothgar's most emotional scene occurs just before Beowulf and his men are ready to depart from Denmark (*Verse 26*). Beowulf offers to come to Hrothgar's assistance when and if he ever needs it and Hrothgar predicts that one day Beowulf will be king of the Geats. Their relationship is more like father and son than king and warrior. Hrothgar realizes that he'll probably never see the young warrior again. He embraces and kisses him, bursting into tears. Some readers feel he's crying not so much because Beowulf is departing, but as a way of releasing all the tension that built up during the years when the Danish people were being tormented by the monsters.

Hrothgar's generosity and dignity are the human counterparts to the violence of the battles between Beowulf and the monsters. He is the model against whom all the other kings and warriors in the poem must be compared.

Wiglaf

As a character, Wiglaf is of tremendous importance to the overall structure of the poem. He's the young warrior who helps Beowulf, the aging king, in his battle against the dragon, in much the same way the younger Beowulf helped king Hrothgar in part one. In this sense Wiglaf is the link between the two parts of the poem. He's also a perfect example of the idea of *comitatus*, the loyalty of the warrior to his leader. While all his fellow warriors flee in fear, Wiglaf alone comes to the aid of his king.

Wiglaf is described by the poet as being of Swedish descent. He's the son of Wextan, and it's with his father's sword that he wounds the dragon. He enters the battle fearlessly, ignoring the dragon's flames when they engulf his armor. But he's not only brave; he has his head on his shoulders as well. Instead of attempting to strike the dragon's head, he pierces the dragon "lower down," sapping its strength so much that Beowulf—with one blow of his sword—is able to sever its head.

Wiglaf plays the role of Beowulf's son, in much the same way Hrothgar performed the role of Beowulf's father. Even though he's filled with grief at the death of his king, he's still able to sound clear-headed and dignified when he addresses his cowardly comrades. Like the young Beowulf, he's a model of self-control, determined to act in a way that he believes is right.

Unferth

The name Unferth means "strife" (un-peace), and when we first meet this character he certainly seems to be living up to his name. A courtier in King Hrothgar's court, he's jealous of Beowulf, and drunkenly accuses the young hero of foolishly risking his life in a swimming match with Brecca years before. He's anxious to dent Beowulf's self-confidence, and tells the hero that his luck will change when he goes up against Grendel.

Beowulf responds by telling the correct version of his swimming match with Brecca. He taunts Unferth, accusing him of cowardice for not defeating Grendel himself, and for having killed his own brother.

Later the poet mentions Unferth in connection with Hrothulf, the king's nephew, implying that Unferth is connected with Hrothulf's ambition to seize the throne after Hrothgar's death. He appears in the poem a third time, as Beowulf is about to descend into the lake to battle with Grendel's mother. Unferth, obviously impressed by Beowulf's strength against Grendel, presents Beowulf with his sword, called Hrunting, as a sign of reconciliation. (Beowulf accepts the gift, but the sword proves useless against the monster.)

We last see Unferth as Beowulf is about to depart from Denmark. Once again he offers the hero his sword as a gift, and Beowulf, not wanting to leave Denmark with any ill feeling, accepts it, making it clear to Unferth that he's forgiven him for his jealous outburst.

What is Unferth's relevance to the story? As a typical warrior of the time—yet one not frightened to speak his mind—he must be seen purely in relation to Beowulf. By presenting an opponent to the young hero, the poet reveals Beowulf's strength of character, his generosity, and his capacity for forgiveness. If Unferth considered himself, and was considered by others, a brave warrior, how much more courageous Beowulf must seem in comparison.

Grendel

Grendel, the first of the three monsters Beowulf kills, lives in the bottom of a lake, or mere, not far from Herot, the great hall that Hrothgar built to house his warriors. According to the poet, the monster is a descendant of Cain, one of many monsters whom God punished for the crime of Abel's death.

Grendel is hostile to humanity. He's inspired to attack Herot after hearing the joyous singing of the warriors. He is enormous, possessing superhuman strength, and appears only at night. For twelve years he has terrorized Denmark, bringing suffering and misery to Hrothgar and his warriors.

Like the Devil, to whom he's often compared, Grendel is an extreme example of evil and corruption. He possesses no human feelings except hatred and bitterness toward mankind. Unlike human beings, however, who can contain elements of good and evil, there's no way Grendel can ever be converted to goodness. As much as he stands for a symbol of evil, he also represents disorder and chaos—a projection of what was most frightening to the Anglo-Saxon mind.

Other Elements

THEMES

1. GOOD AND EVIL

The conflict between good and evil is the poem's most important theme. The poet makes it clear, however, that good and evil don't exist as mutually exclusive opposites, but that both qualities are present in everyone. Beowulf represents the potential to do good—to perform acts selflessly and in the service of others—while Grendel, Grendel's mother, and the dragon are consumed with the blind desire to act against people and to destroy them.

Yet pride, a human quality, is also a sign that evil exists. It's important, as Hrothgar points out to Beowulf, to protect oneself against feeling self-satisfied; you must not ignore the powers to do good with which you've been blessed. The transitoriness and instability of human existence make it essential that you never feel too self-important about what you've done.

The poet also makes clear our need for a code of ethics. Such a code allows members of society to relate to one another with understanding and trust. The most important bond in Anglo-Saxon society was the relation between king and warrior. When the Geat warriors break the bond by refusing to assist Beowulf in his battle with the dragon, the foundation of society collapses, and chaos rules.

2. THE INFLUENCE OF CHRISTIANITY

Beowulf is a link between two traditions, the pagan and the Christian. The virtues of courage in war and the acceptance of feuds between men and countries as a fact of life stem from the older pagan tradition. Beowulf is buried in accordance with pagan ritual. (Note that the poet, obviously a Christian himself, makes no adverse comment on Beowulf's cremation.) When Hrothgar and his counselors turn to their stone gods in an attempt to rid the country of Grendel, the poet makes it clear that idol worshiping is a definite threat to Christianity.

Beowulf, himself, is distinctly more generous in nature than the normal warrior of the time, men like Efor and Wulf who care only about the rewards they'll receive for killing their enemies. Though he possesses spiritual strength, Beowulf isn't particularly concerned with Christian virtues like meekness and poverty. He wants to help people, in a Christian way, but his motivation for doing so is complicated. The poet makes no negative comments about Beowulf's eagerness for material rewards and earthly fame, and gives the impression that these attributes were still acceptable, even to an audience of Christians.

Of all the characters in the poem, Hrothgar is perhaps the one who least fits into the old pagan tradition. His sermon to Beowulf on pride, and his ability to express emotions and love, are certainly in keeping with the new morality of Christianity. Though he's still caught up in the feuds, conspiracies, and wars that are going on around him, he ultimately seems more concerned with his belief in God. (Note that the pagans were more inspired by the Old Testament than the New, and that some readers see Hrothgar as modeled after a king in the Old Testament.)

STYLE

The Anglo-Saxon term for poet was *scop*, or "maker." His role was to travel around from court to court, entertaining the warriors and kings with stories of heroes and their adventures. Often he composed these stories very rapidly, choosing from a reservoir of formulas that had been developed by other poets over a long period of time.

The poet depended on a number of stylistic devices, most notably *alliteration*, the repetition of the same sounds or syllables in two or more words in a line. Here's an example of alliterative verse from the Prologue:

> Him oa Scyld gewat   to gescaep-hwile
> fela-hror feran   on Frean waere.

> When his time was come the old king died,
> Still strong but called to the Lord's hands.
> 26–27

Notice that the first line has two alliterative words, *gewat* and *gescaep*. What are the alliterative words in the second line?

The poet also used a stylistic device called the *kenning*, a method of naming a person or thing by using a phrase that signified a quality of that person or thing. A warrior might be described as "the helmet-bearing one," or the ocean might be called "the riding place of the whales." By means of the kenning the poet was able to vary his language, and create new and dazzling word combinations. (Describing every king as a "ring-giver" is an example of the overuse of a particular kenning.) The poet was always aware that his audience knew the outcome of the story he was telling. In order to make the story interesting he had to tell it in a new way.

Another characteristic of the poet's style is his use of *litotes*, a form of understatement, often with negative overtones, which is intended to create a sense of irony. An example of a litote can be found in the poet's description of Beowulf after he returns to Geatland and presents his treasures to Higlac: "Beowulf had brought his king/Horses and treasure—as a man must,/Not weaving nets of malice for his comrades,/ Preparing their death in the dark, with secret,/Cunning tricks" (2165–69). By telling us what Beowulf hasn't done, the poet creates a stronger sense of his heroic nature.

LANGUAGE

Beowulf is written in a dialect known as Old English (also referred to as Anglo-Saxon). Though there are many similarities between Old English and the English we speak today, a knowledge of the earlier dialect is necessary in order to read the original text. This is why *Beowulf* requires a translation, much as if it had been written in a foreign language.

The language of a country often evolves when the country is invaded by people who speak a different dialect. Old English became the language of its time in the early part of the sixth century A.D., following the occupation of the Romans. The language was also affected by the influence of Christianity that occurred when the Roman invasions took place.

Old English is a heavily accented language and its poetry is known for its emphasis on alliteration and rhythm. Each line of *Beowulf* is divided into two distinct half-lines separated by a pause and related by the repetition of sounds. Each half-line contains at least four syllables. Almost no lines in Old English poetry end in rhymes in the conventional sense, but the alliterative quality of the verse gives the poetry its music and rhythm.

The Norman Conquest in A.D. 1066 introduced many French words into the English language. This date marks the start of the period known as Middle

English. It lasted several hundred years and produced very little great literature that was predominately English until the appearance of Chaucer, the author of *Canterbury Tales*, at the end of the thirteenth century. Most of the themes and the dominant verse forms during this period were influenced by the French invasions. When the Tudor king Henry VII took the throne of England in 1485, the language once again began to change, and the English language started to resemble the language we speak today.

POINT OF VIEW

Many of you will feel that the weakest aspect of the poem is the poet's retelling of the same event again and again, especially Beowulf's battle with Grendel. When Beowulf reports the story of his conquests in Denmark to Higlac, he adds no truly significant detail. Nor does Beowulf's view of the battle tell us anything significant about the hero himself. There's almost no difference between Beowulf's version of the story and the poet's.

Notice that the characters in the poem don't talk to each other as we do. There are no real conversations. Most often the characters just deliver speeches to one another. When Hrothgar, for instance, delivers his sermon on pride, the poet gives us no indication of what Beowulf is thinking. When Beowulf tells Higlac about the upcoming feud between the Danes and the Hathobards, the Geat king says nothing in response.

Also notice the way the poet keeps the story moving by leaping quickly from one event to another. His use of historical digressions is similar to the use of flashbacks in movies and novels. In the middle of Beowulf's fight with Grendel, the poet shifts the point of view to the Danes who are sleeping in another part of the hall. We see them in their beds (782), terrified by the sound of Grendel's screams.

Also, during Beowulf's battle with Grendel's mother, the poet shifts from the struggle beneath the surface of the lake to show us the reactions of the warriors waiting on land. In every battle there's an audience looking on. By using this technique the poet can describe the battle as it's actually happening, and give us the reactions of the audience at the same time.

STRUCTURE

The poet's main structural device is to interweave the events of the present and the past. He frequently interrupts the main narrative with historical digressions that relate, both directly and indirectly, to what's taking place in the main story. For instance, the theme of revenge in the Finnsburg Episode (*Verses 16–17*) is linked to the revenge sought by the dragon, and to the revenge of Grendel's mother for her son's death. Some critics use the word *interlacing* to describe this structure.

Both the digressions and the main narrative contain many common elements. All the major events in the poem deal with feuds: man against man, man against monster. The image of the hero—Beowulf himself—stands at the center of the poem like a rock in a whirl-pool, with all the various stories swirling around him.

The poem is also structured around the theme of youth and age. In part one we see Beowulf as the young, daring prince, in contrast with Hrothgar, the wise but aging king. In part two Beowulf, as the aging but still heroic warrior, is contrasted with his young

follower, Wiglaf. Part of the magic of reading *Beowulf*
is to see the way the two parts parallel one another so
accurately, and how all the major events in the poem
reflect and echo one another.

The Epic Poem

When reading *Beowulf* it's important to see it as part
of the tradition of epic poetry that began with the
poems of Homer—*The Iliad* and *The Odyssey*—and
with Virgil's *Aeneid*. (Whether the *Beowulf* poet himself was familiar with these epics isn't known.) All
these poems deal with the affairs and deeds of brave
men, and focus on the exploits and adventures of one
man in particular. Note that epic poetry usually concerns a few events in the life of a single person; it
makes no attempt to portray a whole life chronologi-
cally from beginning to end.

The epic poet treats all his subjects fairly and objec-
tively. He presents his characters as they are—in realistic fashion—and as they ought to be. Occasionally
he breaks the objective tone to offer a moral judgment
on one of his characters. For the most part, however,
he lets the actions of the characters speak for themselves. Scenes such as the voyages of the Geats to
Denmark (and then home again) and the giving of
rewards for acts of bravery are typical scenes—"set
pieces"—of almost all epic writing.

The epic poet is concerned with human values and
moral choices. The characters are capable of performing acts of great courage; they are also capable of suffering intensely for their deeds. Some of you will feel
that Beowulf is a mixture of both tragedy and comedy,
and that its hero is ultimately a tragic figure. Others of
you will find fault in *Beowulf* for its lack of humor. As
you read the poem, try to notice characters and events

that could be described as being either tragic or comic.

The epic poet also functions as a historian, blending past, present, and future in a unique, all-encompassing way. His pace is leisurely, and allows him to include as many different stories as possible. Remember that the scop's success as an entertainer depended on his ability to re-create these stories in a new way. In *Beowulf* the poet is both telling a story and connecting it to events that have taken place in the past. *Beowulf* is not just a simple tale about a man who kills monsters and dragons, but a large-scale vision of human history.

SOURCES

Although the poem originates in England, it doesn't deal specifically with Anglo-Saxon society. Instead it concerns the lives of various Scandinavian tribes, especially the Danes and the Geats. The work is a blend of fact and fiction; there is no evidence that a hero named Beowulf ever existed. (The only character mentioned in any of the chronicles of the period is Higlac, Beowulf's uncle, whose defeat by the Franks in the year 521 is referred to by the French historian Gregory of Tours.)

The Germanic invaders of Britain brought with them numerous stories and folktales they had heard in their wanderings through Europe between the third and sixth centuries. The poet incorporated many of these stories into his poem, most notably the conflicts between Hengest and Finn, and Ingeld and King Hrothgar.

Monsters resembling Grendel and his mother also appear in a number of Scandinavian folk legends of the time. Grendel, however, is described as a descendant of Cain, and this biblical reference links both the Germanic and Christian influences that pervade the poem. Those of you who interpret the dragon as a Christian symbol of evil will want to ask yourselves how much the poet depended on Christian literature as the main source of his poem.

The importance of *Beowulf* lies in the way the poet was able to infuse all these elements and to create out of these various sources a unified and unique work of literature.

Beowulf critics agree that the poem was composed, at the earliest, between 673 and 735. The latest possible date of composition is usually set at 790. By the middle of the eighth century the Danes had invaded England; scholars assume it was unlikely that an Anglo-Saxon would have written a poem sympathetic to the Danes at that time.

Some critics say that the poem originated in either the court of King Aldfrith of Northumbria or the court of King Offa of Mercia, both courts known for their high level of Anglo-Saxon culture. It's also possible, because of the atmosphere of Christianity that pervades the poem, that *Beowulf* was composed in a monastery. Though the earliest manuscript of the poem dates from the year 1000, none of the theories of authorship, date, and place of composition can be definitely. proved.

The Story

PROLOGUE

The Prologue begins with the words "Hear me!", a rousing cry meant to capture the audience's attention. Remember as you read the poem that *Beowulf* was recited orally long before it was ever written down, and that the first performance probably took place in the middle of a great hall or court where people were eating and drinking. The job of the court poet was to educate and entertain, and most of all to keep his audience interested.

Almost immediately the poet introduces the main subject of the poem: the stories of ancient kings and heroes and how they won glory by acts of courage and bravery. We meet Shild, founder of the Danish dynasty, and his son Beo, who inherits his father's throne. Before Shild appeared, the poet tells us, the Danish people were "kingless and miserable." Under his rule they became a great power.

We're entering a world dominated by kings and their warriors. Though Shild is depicted as a "brave king," his fame is based on turning his enemies into slaves, of terrorizing them into submission. His job as king is to protect his people in whatever way he can, and to accumulate as much wealth as possible for his country. He acquires this wealth by plundering the treasuries of his enemies. A successful king is also one who is generous to his warriors, who rewards them with rings and gold in exchange for their loyalty. This bond between king and warrior is known as *comitatus*. ". . . wealth," we learn, "is shaped with a sword" (25).

The poet informs us that Shild overcame enormous obstacles before he became a king: he was abandoned as a child and arrived in Denmark alone.

NOTE: We'll discover later in the poem that Beowulf himself was considered "worthless" when he was young, and that he, too, had to overcome personal difficulties before becoming a great hero. The poet is saying here that it's possible to alter the course of one's life by means of courage, perseverance, strength of character, and will power, that you can become anything—a king, or a president for that matter—if you possess and cultivate these qualities.

The Prologue ends with a description of Shild's funeral. His warriors place his body on the deck of a ship, surround it with helmets, swords, and coats of mail, and set it adrift.

NOTE: The objects of war obviously play an important role in the lives of these people. The ritual of burying someone alongside his most precious possessions is a way of linking the person's life on earth to the afterlife, whether it be heaven or hell. As we read further, we'll see how religion and ritual gave meaning to the lives of the people in Anglo-Saxon times.

VERSE 1

The first verse tells us about the line of Danish kings. Beo, maintaining the same standard of success set by his father, begets a son, Healfdane, who inherits the throne when Beo dies. Healfdane, "a fierce

fighter," fathers three sons—Hergar, Hrothgar, and
Halga the Good—and a daughter, Yrs, who later
becomes wife of Onela, king of Sweden.

NOTE: Historical sources claim that Hergar and
Halga the Good died when they were young. This
explains why Hrothgar, the second son, assumes the
throne upon Healfdane's death.

Hrothgar is described as possibly the most successful Danish king so far. As he grows older, after a
happy and successful life, he yearns to build a hall to
house his vast army of warriors. Like most people,
Hrothgar desires some outward show of his greatness, a monument that will live on after he dies. The
building of this hall, called Herot, is one way of
achieving immortality.

Notice the way the poet comments on the story,
foreshadowing events in the distant future. Herot is
completed, but to think that it will last forever is an
illusion:

> That towering place, gabled and huge,
> Stood waiting for time to pass, for war
> To begin, for flames to leap as high
> As the feud that would light them, and for Herot
>   to burn.
>
> (82–85)

Eventually another war will break out, the poet
says, and Herot, like everything else, will be destroyed.

The great hall is built. Hrothgar prepares a festive
banquet for his warriors. The court poet entertains the
warriors with songs of the creation of the earth, recall-
ing how the Almighty shaped "These beautiful plains
marked off by oceans,/Then proudly setting the sun

and moon/To glow across the land and light it" (93–95). All is well—or seems to be. Then, as now, we live in a time of contrasts, where the best of times, as Charles Dickens wrote, is also the worst of times. As the festivities at Herot continue night after night, a powerful monster named Grendel is awakened by the carousing of Hrothgar and his men. Grendel hates the idea that people on earth can be happy, and the sound of the men celebrating—especially the poet playing on his harp—stirs him into action.

NOTE: Notice the Christian motifs that run through the poem, and how they contrast with the pagan system of values that underlies the actions of the kings and the warriors. The influence of Christianity was just beginning to make its mark in this world, and most of the characters are torn between their newly discovered religious feelings and their old, heathen way of perceiving things. The idea that there's a higher being that controls one's actions revolutionized people's concepts of themselves, and infused their day-to-day lives with a sense of wonder.

We see Grendel lurking in the shadows, a creature in exile, banished by God.

NOTE: The poet leaves it up to your imagination to supply your own image of a monster. You might compare him to other "monsters"—like King Kong—who have become part of recent American folklore. Grendel walks, thinks, and has a hand and a mouth. He has human qualities but he's also larger than life, capable, as we'll soon learn, of tearing men into pieces and devouring them whole.

VERSE 2

Grendel appears at Herot in the middle of the night. The warriors, sated by drink and food, are "sprawled in sleep," unaware of any imminent danger. Notice that the motif of feasting, followed by going to bed, is another pattern that the poet weaves into the texture of his poem. (In this instance, *bed* means "death.") The monster steals silently into the hall, kills thirty of the sleeping Danish warriors, and returns to his home in the swamp, "delighted with his night's slaughter" (125).

NOTE: At one moment everyone was happy and self-satisfied. How often we've felt that way ourselves, only to be rudely awakened by the harshness of reality! In this case Grendel acts as the terrible reminder that evil lurks in the world, and that all pleasures exist only in the moment and then pass away.

In the morning, Hrothgar, stunned by the loss of his friends, weeps inconsolably, uncertain whether Grendel's attack is just an isolated incident or whether, as the poet says, "the beginning might not be the end." You might think that Grendel would be satisfied with his first night's work, but his hatred of mankind is insatiable. When he returns a second time, the Danish warriors make no attempt to fight against him. It's every man for himself: the only way to escape death is to flee.

NOTE: Doesn't it seem that the Danish warriors, whose reputations depend so much on their courage in the face of danger, should attempt to defend their hall? When we meet Beowulf himself later in the poem, we'll realize the difference between the Danish soldiers, who are ultimately just ordinary mortals like ourselves, and a true hero, for whom no danger is too great.

Twelve years pass. Herot, built as a symbol of Hrothgar's success as a king, remains empty. The story of Grendel, and of Hrothgar's inability to restrain the monster's wrath, spreads across the seas, and is sung "in all men's ears." Grendel appears everywhere, stalking the Danish warriors, lurking in the shadows. At night he lives in Herot, where only Hrothgar's throne, protected by God ("whose love Grendel could not know"), remains unharmed.

Hrothgar and his counselors make useless attempts to appease the monster. They can't offer him gold or land, as they might an ordinary enemy. Like most people in a time of crisis they slip back into old ways of thinking. Instead of praying to God for support, they sacrifice to the stone idols of their pagan past. Though enlightened by Christianity, the poet is saying, pagan rituals were still very much a part of these people's lives.

VERSES 3–4

News of the problems in Denmark have traveled far and wide. Beowulf, a member of the Geat tribe, and described by the poet as "greater/And stronger than anyone anywhere in this world" (195–96), commandeers a boat, enlists fourteen of the strongest and most courageous members of his tribe, and sets sail for the Danish shore.

NOTE: Notice that Hrothgar doesn't ask for help from Beowulf—or from anyone else, for that matter—but that the Geat warrior takes it upon himself to come to the aid of the Danish people. Is Beowulf truly acting selflessly, or is he using the situation to enhance his reputation as the world's bravest man? Later in the poem we'll learn more about Beowulf's character, and get a clearer sense of what makes him tick.

The Geats arrive safely in Denmark, moor their ship, and thank God for a calm voyage. They're greeted by a Danish soldier who's patrolling the cliff above the shore, and who demands to know where they came from and who they are. The soldier is diplomatic, defensive, and most especially curious, because in his own words no one has ever entered Danish territory "more openly" than the Geats. It quickly becomes apparent to him that the Geats have come to help the Danes, not to rob or attack them. They are open because their intentions are honorable; they have nothing to hide. The more open you are, the poet seems to be saying, the more people will trust you.

Beowulf responds to the Danish soldier bluntly and with great self-confidence. He identifies himself as a Geat, a follower of Higlac, and the son of Edgetho. He assures the bewildered soldier that there's nothing ill-intentioned about the purpose of his visit. Talking to the soldier, Beowulf manages to be both dignified and boastful at the same time. (The ability to resolve contradictory elements in one's personality is a trademark, we learn, of the heroic character.) He's obviously someone who believes in himself and wants others to believe in him as well.

NOTE: Outward appearances are important to both the Geats and the Danes. Throughout the poem we read detailed descriptions of the armor and weapons of the soldiers. When the Danish watchman finally offers to lead the Geats to Herot, we see their "golden helmets" on top of which "wild boar heads gleamed." The animal embossed on the helmet gives the warrior an additional form of protection; it's almost as if the animal is with him as he marches into battle. Weapons and armor not only have functional purposes for these people, but possess magical properties as well.

VERSES 5–6

On their way to Hrothgar's palace, the Geats are stopped by a Danish warrior, Wulfgar, who also asks them to identify themselves. At this point the action of the poem has slowed down considerably. Beowulf steps forth a second time, identifies himself and his men, and requests an audience with Hrothgar. Wulfgar is satisfied that the visitors are well intentioned—it's hard not to be impressed by the nobility of their weapons and armor—and encourages Hrothgar to receive them.

NOTE: The conversations between Beowulf and the watchman, and between Beowulf and Wulfgar, are obviously repetitive. There are many such instances throughout the poem where the poet repeats himself, often telling the same incident from different points of view. When this occurs, ask yourself whether this technique adds or detracts from the drama of the story. Is it necessary for Beowulf to introduce himself twice, and yet a third time, even more elaborately, when he finally meets Hrothgar? What do the speeches reveal about Beowulf's character?

His willingness to endure the questions of the king's intermediaries reveals an ability to comply with the formalities of any given situation. Be patient, not arrogant, the poet is telling us, and you'll get what you want.

All the speeches in the poem resemble the lines spoken by an actor or actress in a play. It's important to remember that the poem was first recited orally, and that the performer acted each part to the best of his ability.

Though suspicious of strangers, the Danes are an intuitive people. Wulfgar is described as being famous not only for his strength and courage, but also for his wisdom. Wisdom, in this case, might be defined as an understanding of human nature.

Hrothgar tells Wulfgar that he knew Beowulf when he was a boy. He senses that Beowulf's arrival is a sign that the luck of the Danes is changing, and that God is now acting in their favor. Beowulf's prowess as a warrior is well known, and Hrothgar is confident that he'll be able to defeat Grendel.

Beowulf's speech to Hrothgar is a combination of youthful boastfulness and an understanding that, as one critic has put it, "the wages of heroism is death." It's his self-proclaimed mission in life to enter into situations where death is a possibility. He's also aware that it's ultimately up to God whether he achieves success against Grendel or whether he's killed by the monster.

NOTE: Beowulf's character embodies the major conflict of his times—the conflict between the old pagan rituals and the influence of Christianity. Recall the definition of epic poetry, and ask yourself whether Beowulf's personality conforms to the definition of the epic hero.

There's nothing offensive about Beowulf's boastfulness; he's merely stating what he believes to be true, almost as if he were talking about another person. Telling Hrothgar about his past exploits as a warrior against the Geats' enemies and as a hunter of sea monsters, he's presenting the king with his credentials. Fighting Grendel is a job he feels he was born to do. If he has any doubts about himself, he's not going to reveal them at this moment.

VERSE 7

Hrothgar's response to Beowulf reveals something we didn't previously know: years before, Hrothgar befriended and helped Edgetho, Beowulf's father. We can assume that Beowulf knew about his father's past relationship with the Danish king, and that consequently his instinct to travel to Denmark didn't occur in a vacuum. Part of his incentive—besides the opportunity to rise to new heights of fame and glory—is to repay an old debt.

Hrothgar's modesty, which he reveals when he recounts how he helped Edgetho, acts as a perfect foil for Beowulf's self-confidence. The old, wise king is contrasted with the brash, young warrior. Hrothgar represents a mirror-image, or model, of what Beowulf's own future might be.

The brief story of Edgetho and Hrothgar is the first of many historical digressions that interrupt the flow of the narrative. According to Hrothgar, Edgetho became embroiled in a feud with a tribe called the Wulfings, but Edgetho's countrymen were frightened of going to war. Edgetho turned to the Danes for help, and Hrothgar, a young man "new to the throne," sent treasures to the Wulfings to appease them and end the quarrel. (Notice as you read the poem the many different ways that feuds or disagreements can be resolved.)

Hrothgar passes abruptly from the story of his friendship with Edgetho to a description of the present troubles with Grendel. Though he doesn't say so directly, he implies that Beowulf will be given the chance to prove his courage against the monster. Hrothgar tells Beowulf of all the Danish warriors who have died—foolishly and drunkenly—in an attempt to rid the country of the evil monster.

NOTE: Does Hrothgar's response to Beowulf's arrival seem too restrained, considering what's at stake? How do you think you'd act under similar circumstances?

VERSES 8–9

Verse 8 introduces the character of Unferth, one of Hrothgar's main courtiers, and the son of Eclaf.

During the banquet that follows the arrival of the Geats, Unferth, jealous of Beowulf's reputation and insecure about his own, publicly accuses the visitor of acting foolishly during a swimming match with Brecca, chief of a tribe known as the Brondings. According to Unferth, Beowulf not only lost the match, he needlessly risked his life. Unferth implies that Beowulf's successes so far have been the result of good luck, not strength or courage, and that the young Geat warrior will need more than luck if he expects to defeat Grendel.

Beowulf isn't threatened by Unferth's assault on his character. He accuses Unferth of having had too much to drink. He refutes the Danish courtier's version of the story, and uses the episode to extol his own bravery. He says that both he and Brecca knew they were risking their lives, but were too young to know better. For five days, he says, the two young warriors swam together side by side, each of them carrying a sword to protect them from the whales and the needlefish. Then a flood separated the two rivals, and Beowulf was attacked by a monster who dragged him toward the bottom of the sea where Beowulf pierced its heart with his sword. (Compare this scene with Beowulf's underwater battle with Grendel's mother later in the poem.)

Beowulf escapes one sea monster only to be surrounded by others. The poet describes Beowulf offering the edge of his "razor-sharp sword" to the monsters:

> But the feast, I think, did not please them, filled
> Their evil bellies with no banquet-rich food,
> Thrashing there at the bottom of the sea
>
> (562–64)

Note how the images of "feasting" and "battle" are intertwined throughout the poem.

Beowulf's tone is lighthearted as he describes his escape from the monsters. His self-confidence sometimes seems overwhelming. He sees himself fighting alone, a single individual against the evil in the world. It's not so much that he has faith in God, but that because of his courage, God has faith in him.

After his digression about the sea monsters, Beowulf addresses Unferth directly, accusing him of murdering his brothers and allowing Grendel to ravage his country. He predicts that Unferth's soul will "suffer hell's fires . . . forever tormented." What right, Beowulf asks, does Unferth have to question *his* courage, when Unferth himself has done nothing to end Grendel's reign of terror? He calls the Danes a passive nation ("the quiet Danes") compared to the Geats. In each of his speeches Beowulf appears to be working himself up to his eventual meeting with Grendel.

Hrothgar has been listening to the confrontation between Unferth and Beowulf. He has succumbed to Beowulf's boastfulness and charm, certain, now, that the young warrior will fulfill his promise. The atmosphere in the hall, despite the impending battle, is full of good feelings. You have the impression that Unferth has challenged other visitors in the same way, and that the Danish warriors do not take him very seriously.

Queen Welthow, Hrothgar's wife, "a noble woman who knew/What was right" (*614*), makes her first appearance in the middle of this scene. Despite her aristocratic bearing, her job is to offer mead—a mixture of alcohol, honey, and water—to her husband and his warriors. When the poet describes her as a woman "who knew what was right," he means, in effect, that she knows her place among men. Indeed, the poet's description of Welthow as a "gold-ringed queen" or a "bracelet-wearing queen" gives us the impression of a mannequin rather than a living human being.

After Welthow fills his cup, Beowulf takes the occasion to boast once again of his determination to defeat Grendel. The ritual of accepting the cup from Welthow, however, gives him added incentive. The agreement between Beowulf and the Danish people has been formalized at last, much in the same way two people might sign a legal document or contract.

There are two alternatives: Beowulf will either defeat the monster, or die in the process. "Let me live in greatness/And courage," he says, "or here in this hall welcome/My death!" (636–38).

As the banquet draws to a close, Hrothgar embraces the Geat warrior, and promises him great treasures if he meets with success.

VERSE 10

Hrothgar and his warriors leave the hall, and Beowulf begins to prepare himself for his battle against Grendel. As the time grows near, the outcome of the battle is placed clearly in God's hands. It's God who sent Beowulf to Herot to protect the Danes, and it's God, as well, who will ". . . reward/Whom He chooses!" (687).

Beowulf removes his armor: his mailshirt, his helmet, his sword. He feels that he can easily kill the monster without the weapons—that Grendel, with his claws, teeth, and clumsy fists, is no match against his sword. Killing the monster isn't the only issue at stake in Beowulf's mind. The more risk involved, the

more fame and glory he will receive if he succeeds.
Possibly the monster, Beowulf exclaims, seeing a warrior with no weapons, will be so shocked that his
heart will fail him! Beowulf's confidence in himself is
so great that he's even capable of feeling sympathy for
the monster. He wants the battle to be as fair as possible.

The other Geat warriors, assembled around him in
their various beds, do not share Beowulf's boundless
self-confidence. They fall asleep thinking of all the
Danish warriors whom Grendel has already mur-
dered, and wondering if they'll ever return home
safely. The poet reassures his audience at this point by
revealing the outcome:

> But God's dread loom
> Was woven with defeat for the monster, good for-
>   tune
> For the Geats; help against Grendel was with
>   them,
> And through the might of a single man
> They would win.
>   (696–99)

The juxtaposition of the lines, in this anticipatory
verse, is essential to the tension of the narrative.
Though God is on the side of the Geats, Grendel is
still lurking outside; the battle is still to come. The poet
gives reassurance without lessening the sense of danger. While the Geat warriors lie in their beds, tossing
restlessly, thinking of the friends and homes they left
behind, and as Beowulf lies wakeful, "eager to meet
his enemy," the monster begins his walk in the darkness. Knowing the outcome of the battle doesn't
make the scene any less terrifying.

VERSES 11–12

We see Grendel coming from a distance, over the hills and bogs, half hidden by the mist. He knows his way to Herot, the poet tells us; he's been here before. He, too, is filled with self-confidence, not realizing what awaits him, or that this will be his last visit to the great hall.

He tears the door from its hinges and strides across the threshold. He sees the sleeping warriors and snatches one of them from his bed, ripping the warrior apart, and literally eating him, bit by bit: "death/ And Grendel's great teeth came together,/Snapping life shut" (743–45). This scene is described in great vividness, but it leaves us with the question of why Beowulf, lying awake in his own bed nearby, would allow Grendel to kill one of his men. This inability to act more quickly seems irresponsible on Beowulf's part. Is one person's life less important than any other?

Perhaps there's a logic to Beowulf's thinking. Watching Grendel devour the Geat warrior gives him time to assess the strength of his enemy. Killing one warrior, the monster probably assumes that he'll be able to devour them all, that no one will dare to challenge him. If you could read Grendel's mind he'd probably be thinking that this night at Herot will be no different from any other, and that he'll have free run of the hall, just like the time before. Beowulf obviously feels that the element of surprise—catching Grendel off-guard—is worth the price of the life of one of his comrades.

Grendel approaches Beowulf's bed and clutches at him with his claws. This is the moment Beowulf has been waiting for. He instantly strikes back, bending

the monster's claws and cracking them in his fist.
Grendel realizes almost immediately that he's met his
match; his first impulse is to flee and return to his
home in the swamp. Is it surprising that Grendel,
after all we've heard about him, succumbs so easily?

Grendel tries to escape from Beowulf's grip. His
shrieks of pain awaken the Danish warriors. The
other Geat warriors leap from their beds, their swords
raised, none of them knowing that Grendel is immune to ordinary weapons. In the middle of the battle
the poet comments on the possible future destruction
of Herot by fire. Even though Beowulf will defeat the
monster, at some time in the future their great hall will
be destroyed, and all of Beowulf's heroics rendered
ultimately meaningless.

NOTE: Notice how the poet varies the point of view
in this section—how we see the action from Grendel's
point of view, through Beowulf's eyes, and through
the poet's own comments on the reactions of the Danish warriors. Shifting the point of view is a technique
used more frequently in novels than in poems. Do
you feel that the technique is successful here?

Beowulf wants to hold onto the monster until it
dies, but Grendel manages to twist free, though not
before losing his arm. The "bloodthirsty fiend" will
escape to his home at the bottom of the swamp,
where he will die and descend to hell, into "the waiting hands of still worse fiends" than even himself.
Much in the same way a hunter hangs a trophy above
his fireplace, so Beowulf hangs Grendel's arm from
the rafters of the hall. It's the unquestionable proof of
what he has done.

NOTE: The drama of the battle is heightened, some readers feel, by the presence of the audience of Geat and Danish warriors. Though we know the outcome, they don't. When the poet describes how "the Danes started/In new terror, cowering in their beds as the terrible/Screams of the Almighty's enemy sang/In the darkness" (783–86), the reader feels the horror of the situation along with them.

VERSE 13

News of Grendel's death spreads quickly. The Danish princes and warriors flock to Herot to inspect the monster's footprints and follow them from the great hall to the edge of the swamp. They stare into the water, "steaming and boiling in horrible pounding waves," as if unable to believe Grendel is finally dead. This is a verse of great celebration, an exultant hymn of praise on behalf of the Danes to Beowulf.

Notice the way the poet describes the Danes as they return to Herot from Grendel's swamp. At first they jog along, slowly, retelling the story of Beowulf's battle with the monster. Then, as their excitement builds, they let their horses run free, "red and brown and pale yellow backs streaming down the road." Finally, one of the king's minstrels bursts into a song of praise, skillfully interweaving Beowulf's triumph over Grendel with the adventures of two other Danish heroes, Siegmund and Hermod.

NOTE: The choice of Siegmund and Hermod is no accident. Siegmund's adventures include a battle with "a treasure-rich dragon," a story that foreshadows Beowulf's own battle with a dragon later in the poem. Both Siegmund and Beowulf, as heroes, are cut from the same mold—they are committed to purge the world of evil and treachery. Hermod, however, is a failed hero. Considered at one time one of "the mightiest of men," he was overcome by vanity and pride. Instead of easing the pain of other people, his exploits only added to their suffering. (Keep this scene in mind when you come to Hrothgar's speech to Beowulf on the dangers of pride.)

Contrasting these warriors, the poet is saying that courage alone is not enough to make a person a hero. The true hero possesses a code of ethics that includes taking other people's feelings into consideration. A warrior like Hermod who acts out of his own self-interest is doomed.

VERSES 14–15

Hrothgar's speech to Beowulf is more than an expression of gratitude. "Let me take you to my heart," he says, "make you my son too,/And love you" (947–48). When a person performs a great favor for you, as Beowulf has done for Hrothgar and the Danes, the immediate, human response is to accept the person into your family. If someone were to save your life wouldn't you feel that way toward her or him? (Remember, too, that Beowulf and Hrothgar are connected by Hrothgar's relationship to Beowulf's father.) Accepting Beowulf as a son is more important than all the material wealth Hrothgar can offer.

NOTE: Again, notice how the influence of Christianity pervades Hrothgar's speech to Beowulf. It was the Almighty who sent Beowulf to Denmark and it was "with the Lord's help" that Beowulf was able to defeat Grendel. Beowulf's mother "knew the grace of the God of our fathers" for giving birth to such a great hero. Do you think that Hrothgar is minimizing Beowulf's achievement by attributing his defeat of Grendel to the will of God?

Beowulf's response is almost apologetic (especially in comparison to his more boastful speeches in the previous verses). Though Grendel is obviously dead, and his severed arm hangs from the rafters, Beowulf isn't completely satisfied with his accomplishment. His retelling of the story of his battle with Grendel is an example of the poet's technique of describing the same scenes from different points of view.

NOTE: The contrast between age and youth, father and son, is one of the major themes of the poem, and the speeches by Beowulf and Hrothgar provide one of the best examples. Although Beowulf is described as being youthful, his exact age is never stated. When he first arrives in Herot he announces to Hrothgar that "the days/Of my youth have been filled with glory" (408–409). He is already known throughout the world as the strongest man alive and a proven hero. It's this quality of agelessness, as if his life were suspended in time, that sets him apart from other men, and defines him as a truly heroic individual.

Notice the poet's ability to describe things with precision. At the start of Verse 14 we see Grendel's claw "swinging high from that gold-shining roof." At the end of the verse the poet returns to the image of the claw:

                                    swinging high
From Hrothgar's mead-hall roof, the fingers
Of that loathsome hand ending in nails
As hard as bright steel

                                            (983–86)

Now that Grendel is dead it's time to prepare a great banquet. The poet takes the opportunity to refer to the battle between Beowulf and Grendel (996) and again we see the monster and the hero wrestling together under Herot's roof. The poet gives momentum to his material by describing the same thing in different ways. In this way he's similar to a jazz musician, improvising the same melody and chords, never repeating himself exactly, but always on the lookout for new ways of stating his themes.

NOTE: The image of the feast (1008) comes up again and again; eating and death are interrelated. Here human life itself is described as a feast. After every banquet the tired warriors go to bed where in the darkness—as we'll see soon enough—they'll meet their death.

Hrothgar and his nephew Hrothulf enter the hall and begin the celebration by toasting each other. The poet points out that for this moment, at least, all the Danes are genuinely happy (1018–19). No one is plotting any new conspiracy. Such unity of good spirits is rare; this moment, like all others, is transitory. Who knows what new horror the next night will bring? And isn't the poet hinting that some future act of treachery will occur? Why does he choose this moment to mention Hrothulf?

VERSES 16–17

More gift-giving is in order. Hrothgar presents armor and swords to all the Geat warriors who accompanied Beowulf on his voyage. For the Geat warrior who was eaten in his sleep by Grendel, Hrothgar gives the Geats gold, presumably to be paid over to the slain warrior's family. Hrothgar's actions are generous and compassionate.

The poet briefly interrupts the narrative to comment on God's role in the battle between Beowulf and Grendel. Both God and Beowulf's own courage are given equal importance in the poet's eyes. People, the poet says, must open themselves to God's power and be aware, whether they like it or not, that both good and evil exist in the world.

The court poet entertains the jubilant warriors with stories and tales from Danish history. He tells of how a band of Danes, under the leadership of Hnaf, are killed—for unspecified reasons—by the followers of the Frisian king, Finn, at his hall in Finnsburg. (Some readers refer to this digression as the Finnsburg Episode.) Both Hnaf and his nephew die in the battle. Hnaf's sister is Finn's wife; she feels her husband betrayed her by attacking her brother, and for starting a battle in which both her brother and her son lost their lives. (Though her identity is not mentioned in the poem, historical sources report that her name is Hildeburh.)

Hengest, Hnaf's follower, refuses to leave the hall. As a gesture of peace, Finn offers to divide the hall with the Danes. Hengest agrees, even though he hates Finn. As part of the agreement Finn promises to punish any of his men who attempt to rekindle the feud.

A funeral pyre is built for the dead warriors. Notice the vividness with which the poet describes the cremation, the way "the greedy fire-demons drank flesh and bones/From the dead of both sides, until nothing was left" (1123–24). Notice, also, the way the poet uses the image of feasting to describe the fire. Compare this funeral with Shild's in the Prologue, and—when you come to it—Beowulf's own funeral at the end of the poem.

All winter Hengest and a few of his men live in the hall at Finnsburg; the sea is too rough for them to return to Denmark. Hengest is torn between his desire for revenge against Finn, and his moral obligation to comply with the peace offering. Though he hates Finn, he still possesses a sense of honor. It's only when spring finally comes that Hengest resolves his inner conflict by killing Finn, ransacking his hall, and taking Hildeburh back to Denmark.

After the court poet finishes his story, Welthow steps forward and advises Hrothgar not to be carried away by his feelings of gratitude toward Beowulf. She's worried that he'll treat Beowulf more like a son than his own sons. She asks Hrothgar to have confidence in Hrothulf, his nephew. She tries to convince him that when he dies his sons "will be safe,/Sheltered in Hrothulf's gracious protection" (1180–81).

The Finnsburg Episode deals with treachery and revenge. Because all the historical digressions have relevance to the main narrative, the poet didn't choose to tell this particular story at this point without good reason. The main characters in the Finnsburg Episode are Hildeburh—whose fate is to be torn apart by her bonds of kinship with the Finns and the Danes—and Hengest, whose code of ethics is upset by the conflict between honor and revenge.

NOTE: In the previous verse the poet let us know that for a rare moment—during the celebration for Beowulf—there was an absence of conspiratorial feelings. Yet treachery, conspiracy, and evil are part of life, and the poet is implying through the Finnsburg Episode that this moment of calm isn't going to last. You might read this section as you would a mystery story, where the author is supplying hints and clues about what's going to happen next.

The most mysterious character in this section is Hrothulf. He's first mentioned in line 1014, at the start of the banquet for Beowulf. Then, as Welthow makes her appearance in the hall after the Finnsburg Episode, he's described sitting "peacefully together" with Hrothgar, "their friendship and Hrothulf's good faith still unbroken" (1164–65). The poet is once again hinting that at some future date Hrothulf will be involved in a conspiracy against the king—that his good faith will be broken and he's not a person to be trusted.

At this moment the poet chooses to mention Unferth, who's sitting at Hrothgar's feet, and to remind us that although "everyone trusted him" no one forgot that "he'd spilled his relatives' blood." The poet is in the process of weaving a very complicated drama involving loyalty and kinship.

The poet intends us to compare Welthow and Hildeburh. Welthow advises Hrothgar to put his faith in Hrothulf—in much the same way Hildeburh put her faith in Finn. The poem at this point is like a tapestry, where all events and stories are interconnected.

VERSE 18

Beowulf is rewarded with yet another gift, "the most beautiful necklace known to men." At a certain point, all these material objects—the swords, the armor, the helmets, the horses, the jewels—seem to lose their value. Do you think the Danes have gone overboard in their expression of thanks toward Beowulf? Is the accumulation of wealth Beowulf's primary concern?

NOTE: By telling us the history of the necklace of the Brosings the poet seems to be mimicking the endless gift-giving. Is any object, he's asking, worth fighting about? The emphasis on objects is connected to the pagan, nonreligious world that existed before the advent of Christianity. Objects are like idols, symbolizing fame and wealth. Beowulf can be seen as the hero of the future. Though he accepts the gifts (fame and wealth are obviously important to him), he's more interested in pleasing God, and he knows that the way to do this is by acting ethically and with concern for others.

Welthow presents Beowulf with these valuable jewels and asks him to lend his strength and wisdom to her two sons. In her speech, the poet reveals her to be innocent of the forces of evil, an uncynical person who believes that among the Danes "men speak softly" and "trust their neighbors." She describes the Danes as "loyal followers who would fight as joyfully as they drink."

Welthow is under the illusion that now that Grendel is dead the world will return to the way it was before. Yet the poet has hinted—in the Finnsburg Episode, especially—that disaster and unexpected turns of fate are facts of life. Nothing can be taken for granted.

The soldiers fall asleep as they did after the first banquet. Again, the poet foreshadows the theme of "bed after feast." He implies that something terrible is about to happen. By now we must realize that the world described by the poet is in a constant state of change, passing from exultation to tragedy in the course of a day.

VERSE 19

It's the middle of the night and all the warriors, both Danes and Geats, are asleep. Beowulf and his men aren't sleeping in the great hall, however, but "had been given better beds." By now we can expect almost anything to happen. All the drama of the last few verses has been directed toward this moment.

The main theme of the Finnsburg Episode was revenge. Now Grendel's mother appears—from out of the same swamp where her son had lived—to avenge her loss on the inhabitants of Herot.

Once again the poet tells the battle between Grendel and Beowulf.

NOTE: Are all these repetitions of the same event necessary? Let's assume that the poet in the oral telling of the story backtracked every few verses to remind his audience of what had happened. Also, when you tell someone a story it's often natural to repeat some things in a different way for emphasis. Some critics feel the repetitions detract from the poem while others think they add to the tension. This is something you'll have to decide for yourself.

The visit from Grendel's mother, the poet tells us, ended the good fortune of the Geats. It seems only a few hours have passed since Grendel's death, enough time for another banquet.

NOTE: Is the poet being overly moralistic here? Every time you truly enjoy yourself, he's saying, something horrible happens to you. It's a mistake to feel too self-confident, too sure of yourself. Evil— whether it takes the form of a monster or a treacherous warrior—is always in the air.

Grendel's mother enters the hall where the warriors are sleeping. (Why do you think the Danes neglected to post any soldiers at the door of Herot?) They wake in time to ward off the attack with their swords but the monster manages to escape with one victim in her claws. The poet, again, leaves it up to your imagination to visualize Grendel's mother.

After she escapes, the warriors realize that she managed to steal back Grendel's claw from where it was hanging on the rafters. The victim turns out to be one of Hrothgar's closest advisers, "the man he loved most of all men on earth." The king summons Beowulf and his men. There's a feeling of desperation in the air, but as Beowulf walks through the halls of Herot on his way to the king's throne, he "Rehearsed the words he would want with Hrothgar;/He'd ask the Danes' great lord if all/Were at peace, if the night had passed quietly" (1318–20). We know Beowulf realizes that something is dreadfully wrong—no doubt he can hear the uproar from the main hall—but he also knows that it's his job to convey confidence and self-control. At this moment the young warrior seems wiser and more mature than the aging king.

VERSE 20

Hrothgar is beside himself. "Anguish," he tells Beowulf, "has descended on the Danes." It's surprising, in a way, that the king is so shocked. In the course of his speech we learn that, in fact, Grendel had been seen in the company of another monster. Why didn't the Danes expect this other creature to appear one day?

Hrothgar's speech to Beowulf contains a description of the swamp, or "mere," where Grendel's mother lives. The description is realistic and dreamlike at the same time. The trees growing over the lake "are covered with frozen spray." A deer pursued by hunters would prefer to die on the shore of the lake rather than seek shelter and safety in the water. During storms, "waves splash toward the sky,/As dark as the air, as black as the rain/That the heavens weep" (1374–76). It's the poet's ability to evoke a landscape or scene, as much as his insight into human nature, that has established *Beowulf's* place in the tradition of great literature.

The king begs Beowulf to help him once again. He's visibly shaken by the death of his friend Esher. His speech displays the capacity and depth of his feelings. Of everyone in the poem, Hrothgar is the person most capable of relating to the events in the world in a way that is truly human.

VERSES 21–23

Beowulf's heroic stature is never more in evidence than when he consoles Hrothgar on the death of his friend, and offers to kill Grendel's mother. Both men follow the monster's tracks until they reach the lake where the monsters live and where now, floating on the water, they see "Esher's bloody head."

NOTE: Some readers interpret the poet's use of the image of dismemberment—Grendel's claw, Esher's head—as a metaphor for the disunity in the world. A person's body, they say, is like a world in itself. Protecting the body with armor and helmets is a way of protecting one's world.

The surface of the lake is swarming with serpents and sea monsters. Beowulf, for no apparent reason, shoots an arrow at one of the monsters. What does he have to prove? Remember the earlier story of his swimming match with Brecca and how he boasted of his ability to fight against sea monsters. Possibly in this instance he is merely testing himself, as a way of preparing for his underwater battle with Grendel's mother.

He has certainly proved his courage to Unferth. No longer doubting Beowulf's superhuman abilities, he gives the hero a special sword to take into battle. Is Unferth reconciled to the fact that Beowulf is a braver warrior than he? He does seem genuinely embarrassed by the speech he made when Beowulf first arrived in Denmark. Beowulf, by killing Grendel, has revealed to the Danish warriors the limits of their own bravery; all they can do is stand back, awestruck, as he prepares to enter the lake.

Beowulf tells Hrothgar that if he dies in the lake to look after his comrades and to send his treasures to Higlac, king of the Geats. Beowulf again reveals the aspects of his personality that make him a true hero: consideration of others, humility, generosity, and awareness of his own mortality.

Without waiting for a response from Hrothgar, Beowulf leaps into the snake-infested waters. "For hours he sank through the waves," the poet says, indicating that Beowulf possesses the amazing power to hold his breath underwater for an unlimited period of time. Some readers feel that this ability detracts from the realistic nature of the story, and gives the impression that Beowulf is more like a good monster than a man. (It has been suggested that in keeping with the Christian themes that pervade the poem, Beowulf's descent into the lake represents a true descent into the underworld or hell.)

Grendel's mother captures Beowulf in her claws and drags him down to her cave at the bottom of the lake. As they wrestle together, the other sea monsters look on—in much the same way the Geat and Danish warriors watched as Beowulf battled Grendel. Beowulf attempts to sever the monster's head with Unferth's sword before realizing that Grendel's mother, like her son, is immune to ordinary weapons, and that "no sword could slice her evil skin."

Beowulf, the poet tells us, is motivated by his desire for fame, as if he didn't have enough already. "So fame/Comes to the men who mean to win it/And care about nothing else!" (1534–36). The desire for revenge that motivates Grendel's mother makes her seem even fiercer than her son. Remember that Grendel didn't put up much of a fight against Beowulf, while Grendel's mother, "squatting with her weight on his stomach," almost manages to stab Beowulf with her dagger.

Until the very end of Verse 22 there's no mention of God's help. Beowulf in this battle is relying on courage alone. But when all is hopeless, and Grendel's mother appears to have the upper hand, God intervenes. It's as if God has been looking on all along, waiting for the right moment to show whose side He's on.

The battle ends swiftly. Beowulf sees the magic sword hanging on the wall of the cave, and in a moment of desperation and pure strength, cuts off the monster's head. A brilliant light shines through the roof of the monsters' hall, a supernatural light "as bright as heaven's own candle." Recall that in the simplest sense evil is associated with darkness (Grendel and his mother appear only at night) and goodness with light.

The poet then retells the story of Grendel's attacks, creating a bridge between the two battles. Beowulf explores the monsters' hall, finds Grendel's body, and cuts off his head.

NOTE: Revenge, which motivates the people in this society, is not to be taken lightly. Recall the Finnsburg Episode, and how a feud between tribes could be resolved only by taking revenge for what the other tribe had done. Is revenge ("an eye for an eye") the great equalizer? Is the poet telling us that no true resolution can take place without it?

We return to the audience of warriors standing at the edge of the lake. As the blood (it's Grendel's mother's blood, but they don't know that yet) rises to the surface, they begin to lose all hope that the Geat hero will ever return. "Almost all agreed that Grendel's/Mighty mother, the she-wolf, had killed him" (1598–99). Hrothgar and his men give up and go home, while Beowulf's comrades linger. Does it surprise you, after all Beowulf has accomplished, that they give up hope so easily?

The poet takes us from the real world—the warriors awaiting the news of Beowulf's fate—to the supernatural underwater world where Beowulf is battling the monsters. The sword, without which Beowulf would certainly have died, begins melting away like an icicle: it dissolves "in Grendel's steaming blood." The sword is the sign of God's presence. Beowulf takes Grendel's head and the hilt of the magical sword, and swims up to the surface to rejoin his comrades.

VERSES 24–25

In his triumphant speech to Hrothgar on his return to Herot, Beowulf attributes his success against Grendel's mother to "God's guidance." He realizes that without the magic sword he might have lost his life. Again the poet backtracks and, in Beowulf's voice, retells the story of finding the sword and killing the monster.

NOTE: The relationship between Grendel and his mother is one of kinship and parallels the many blood relationships that the poet describes throughout his story.

In the ancient letters, "runes," written on the hilt of the magic sword, the old king reads the battle between good and evil and the history of the evil giants. Then Hrothgar, realizing that Beowulf's work in Denmark is over, warns the Geat hero against letting his successes and fame go to his head. He advises Beowulf not to become like Hermod, the Danish leader whose story the poet has already told us (900). Hermod abused his power, brought destruction to his people, and ended his life alone and friendless.

It's up to God, Hrothgar tells Beowulf, to grant men wisdom, greatness, and wealth. Yet once a person has power and fame he must learn how to use it correctly. A prosperous person forgets that he's been blessed with God's favor. He allows pride, devilish pride, to grow in his heart and soul. Before he knows it his body fails him; it's too late to make amends for the evil things he's done. The greatest evil, we learn, is not taking advantage of God's favor. If he gives you wealth or power, use it well. If you don't you'll die alone, bitter, and filled with regret.

Death is inevitable, Hrothgar tells Beowulf, even for the greatest of warriors.

How closely is Beowulf listening to Hrothgar's sermon? The great hero doesn't respond and for the moment we have no way of knowing what he's thinking. Hrothgar's speech ends with the promise of more treasures—possibly that's what Beowulf is really interested in.

The warriors sit down to yet another feast, a farewell dinner because the next morning the Geat warriors plan to begin their voyage home. There's a feeling of peace and serenity in the hall. The warriors can finally all go to bed without the fear that some new danger lurks in the shadows.

Eating, sleeping, gift-giving—these scenes seem to follow a set pattern. First joy occurs, then sorrow. Possibly a new feud will begin the next day or an act of treachery will occur. These people (with the possible exception of Hrothgar) live very much in the present moment; they accept instability and sudden change as a fact of life. From day to day, from night to night, no one knows what to expect.

No monster comes to haunt the great hall in the middle of the night. Instead, "a black-feathered raven" is singing outside the windows.

Except for the raven, the night passes uneventfully. The Geat warriors, anxious to return home, rise early and begin preparing for their voyage. Unferth, still trying to make up with Beowulf after his initial blunder, offers him his sword, Hrunting, as a farewell gift. Beowulf, with Hrothgar's sermon on pride still fresh in his ears, accepts Unferth's gift forgivingly. His words of thanks, the poet tells us, "were spoken like the hero he was!"

VERSE 26

Before leaving, Beowulf returns to Herot to visit the king one last time. His speech shows us clearly that he's taken Hrothgar's sermon to heart. His modesty and generosity are as impressive as his self-confidence was earlier. He offers to return with "a thousand armed Geats" if Denmark is ever again threatened by enemies or if the king ever needs his help.

Hrothgar's farewell speech is the most emotional passage in the poem. His ability to express what he's really feeling gives the poem as a whole an added dimension. Through Hrothgar's character the poet is informing us that the people in Anglo-Saxon society are not merely barbarians—going to war, feasting, plotting against one another—but also possess the capacity to care about what their comrades are feeling.

Hrothgar predicts that when Higlac dies Beowulf will surely become the king of the Geats. He kisses Beowulf good-bye and bursts into tears, realizing (he's an old man, after all) that it's possible he'll never see the young warrior again. "His love," the poet tells us, "was too warm to be hidden."

NOTE: Then, as now, people had a hard time expressing their feelings, and some readers think that the poet himself believes that Hrothgar's tears are a sign of weakness. "Winter had followed winter," the poet tells us, "and age had stolen his strength." Do you think the ability to express feelings is a sign of strength or of weakness?

VERSE 27

Loaded down with treasures, the Geats march proudly down to the shore. The same soldier who met them when they arrived in Denmark (*Verse 3*) comments to them that their countrymen will be glad to see them when they return.

Notice the energy and spirit of the language the poet uses to describe the voyage. It's almost as if the words themselves were propelling the boat over the waves. "Driven/By the wind," he writes, "the ship rammed high on the shore" (*1912–13*). The Geats are characterized as an aggressive and forceful tribe, and it's no accident that the poet uses words like *driven* and *rammed* to describe their homecoming.

As the Geats carry their treasures to Higlac's hall, the poet interrupts the narrative with another digression. This one concerns Higd, Higlac's wife and the daughter of Hareth. Higd is "young but wise and knowing beyond her years," a generous queen who happily distributed her husband's wealth among his followers. In contrast, her daughter Thrith is arrogant and destructive, so vicious "that her father's followers/Averted their eyes as she passed" (*1932–33*). More than once a man was executed for staring at her. After Thrith marries Offa, a member of the Hemming tribe, her personality changes radically. Her husband's followers praise her for "her generous heart" and for the "adoring love" she displays for her husband. (Some readers compare Thrith to Katherine in Shakespeare's *The Taming of the Shrew*. Others describe her as a female version of Hermod.) The digression ends with words of praise for Offa.

NOTE: The poet makes us wonder about the relevance of all this to the main narrative. Of course, since Beowulf and his men are about to meet with Higlac, it's only natural that the poet should want to fill us in about the king's family. Perhaps he wants us to compare Offa and Higlac, whom we'll meet for the first time in the next verse. Remember this digression as you read further, and try to see how it connects to the main story.

VERSES 28–30

Does Beowulf's retelling of his exploits in Denmark add anything to our knowledge? Or is it just the poet's way of bringing the story up to date for his audience?

For the first time we see Beowulf at home among friends. We see the hero and his men at the foot of Higlac's throne. And once again we see the queen pouring drinks for the king and his warriors. (Does it seem that pouring drinks for the men and bestowing gifts on the brave warriors are the main functions of women in this society?)

Beowulf makes it clear right from the start that news of his success against Grendel wasn't something that could ever be questioned. Possibly he's thinking of Unferth's remarks about his swimming match with Brecca (*Verse 8*). "Not even the oldest of his evil kind," he reassures Higlac, "will ever boast, lying in sin/And deceit, that the monster beat me" (*2007–2009*).

He interrupts the chronological story of his adventures to tell Higlac a historical digression of his own. This one concerns Freaw, Hrothgar's daughter, whom the king is planning to marry to Ingeld, a prince of the Hathobard tribe, in the hope that this arrangement will settle the quarrel between the Danes and the Hathobards. Beowulf, however, is skeptical about this method of ending the feud. He predicts that on the very day of the wedding, when the Danes and the Hathobards get together, one of Ingeld's soldiers will drunkenly provoke one of the Danes, and the feud between the two tribes will erupt again.

NOTE: All the historical digressions involve feuds between men, but the main narrative concerns feuds between men and monsters. Some critics think that the digressions are the most important sections of the poem and tell us more about the society of these people than Beowulf's heroic battles. It's fun to go back over the poem and read the digressions separately from the main narrative to see how they connect to one another.

From Beowulf's story of his battle with Grendel we learn that the monster had a pouch at his side, "a huge bag sewn/From a dragon's skin" (2086–87). Beowulf tells Higlac that "the monster intended to take me, put me inside, save me for another meal." The image of the pouch is the only detail the poet omitted from his own version of the story. This comment that Beowulf could fit inside the monster's pouch gives us our only concrete idea of the monster's actual size. Or do you think that Beowulf is exaggerating Grendel's physical stature to impress Higlac?

Hrothgar, in Beowulf's words, is a melancholy old man, filled with the memories of the battles he won when he was younger. We see him stroking the strings of a harp, "reciting unhappy truths about good/And evil" (2110–11). We see him weeping at the death of Esher, his closest friend. We see him begging Beowulf to kill Grendel's mother. Do these images of Hrothgar coincide with what we already know about him? Or is Beowulf again altering the picture slightly for Higlac's benefit?

Notice that Beowulf's descriptions of his adventures contain almost no mention of God's help. His remarks at the end of his description of the battle with Grendel's mother that "I had barely escaped/With my life, my death was not written" (2140–41) indicate the concerns with fate, and the power of God to alter man's fate, that existed in Anglo-Saxon society.

VERSE 31

Beowulf ends his speech to Higlac with an avowal of loyalty to his king. "I have almost no family,/ Higlac," he says, "almost no one, now, but you" (2150–51). Describing his adventures in Denmark, he was careful not to praise Hrothgar too highly for fear, perhaps, of offending Higlac. Now he's saying, as a way of reassuring the Geat king, that despite his feelings for Hrothgar he has remained faithful to the Geats. Everything he did in Denmark was to bring honor and glory to his homeland.

Beowulf presents Higlac with his treasures. The poet's brief commentary on Beowulf's character gives us an indication of the feelings of paranoia that pervaded the minds of people in the Anglo-Saxon world:

> Beowulf had brought his king
> Horses and treasure—as a man must,
> Not weaving nets of malice for his comrades,
> Preparing their death in the dark, with secret,
> Cunning tricks.

> (2165–69)

Treachery, malice, hatred—all these are the expected ways of behaving. To act selflessly, and to perform heroically for the sake of one's country, was

obviously rare. No wonder Hrothgar loved Beowulf
so much.

The poet gives us a brief summary of Beowulf's
childhood: how he'd been scorned by his fellow Geats
who "were sure he was lazy, noble but slow." It's
possible that Beowulf's motivation to become a great
warrior was to prove himself to the people who'd
scorned him when he was younger. The need for
respect from our friends and peers is a universal feeling, and certainly one we can all identify with.

This verse marks the transition between Beowulf's
youth and his old age. After Higlac dies and his son
Herdred is killed in battle with the Swedes, Beowulf
takes the throne and rules over the Geat kingdom for
fifty years.

NOTE: The poet tells us little about what occurred
during Beowulf's reign except to say that he held the
throne "long and well." Why do you think the poet
spends only a few lines describing Beowulf's fifty-year
reign, and almost three verses recounting his exploits
in Denmark? Remember that an epic poem usually
concentrates on a few important events in a person's
life, rather than attempting to portray an entire life
from beginning to end.

At the end of his life we learn that a new challenge
has presented itself to Beowulf. Geatland is being terrorized by a fire-breathing dragon who was awakened
when a thief entered his castle and stole a jeweled cup
from his treasure-hoard. The dragon wreaks havoc on
the Geats in much the same way Grendel terrorized
the Danes. It's up to Beowulf as king to protect his
people, and the second part of the poem will be dominated by this final conflict.

VERSE 32

The thief is the first character in the poem who is neither a member of the aristocracy nor a warrior. "He was someone's slave," the poet tells us, reminding us that a society of ordinary people existed outside the great halls and battlefields.

The dragon is guarding a treasure-hoard left by "the last survivor of a noble race," who, before he died, locked his gold and jewels in a stone fortress. "The Lay of the Last Survivor," as it's called (beginning 2247), is one of the most moving speeches in the poem, and recalls Hrothgar's sermon to Beowulf about pride and the transience of fame and wealth. The speech also foreshadows the end of the Geat dynasty, and of all dynasties, and mocks the endless giving of gifts that occurs throughout the first part of the poem.

NOTE: Notice as you read the second part whether the poet's style is different from the first part. Remember that some readers think that the two parts were composed by two different poets.

After the last survivor of this "noble race" finally dies, his treasure-hoard is discovered by a dragon. In the last survivor's speech, the futility of acquiring material objects is emphasized, so it's no surprise that the treasure-hoard is now guarded by a dragon for whom the treasures have absolutely no use. The stealing of a single cup from the hoard only highlights the pettiness and greed of a society that places such a high premium on material wealth.

VERSES 33–35

As Grendel tormented the Danish people in part one, so the dragon vents its anger on the Geats in part two. Like Grendel, the dragon strikes only at night, burning houses so that "the signs of its anger flickered and glowed in the darkness." Nothing is spared, not even Beowulf's hall and throne.

When Beowulf learns that his own house has been destroyed, his first thought is that he did something to anger God, and he feels guilty. (The poet never makes it clear whether an offense against God actually did occur.)

NOTE: Does Beowulf's reaction seem in keeping with what we know about his character? As king his main function is to protect his people. This is different from the role of warrior that he played in part one. Consequently, he himself must accept the blame for all acts of evil that are performed by or against his country. The stealing of the dragon's cup becomes Beowulf's responsibility, whether he likes it or not.

Beowulf prepares to fight the dragon. At this point the poet again foreshadows the outcome of the poem. Beowulf will die soon, the poet tells us, "but would take the dragon/With him, tear it from the heaped-up treasure/It had guarded so long" (2343–45). Beowulf's youth is evoked by a brief retelling of his battles against Grendel and Grendel's mother, and of his exploits fighting side by side with Higlac during the war with the Frisians.

In part two the poet effortlessly blends past and present events. In retelling Beowulf's exploits against the Frisians during which Higlac was killed, the poet

describes Beowulf as "the only survivor," relating him
to "the last survivor" whose treasures fell into the
hands of the evil dragon. The connections between
present events and the historical digressions are much
more evident in part two than in part one.

After the Frisian War Beowulf is offered the leadership of the Geats. He turns it down, however, preferring to support Herdred, Higlac's son, and the
rightful heir to the throne. In the course of his king-
ship, Herdred offers to harbor a group of Swedish
exiles—rebels, we are told, against Onela, the Swedish king. Onela invades Geatland in search of the
rebels, and Herdred is slain, forcing Beowulf to
assume the position he didn't originally want, king of
the Geats. Beowulf leads the Geat army in a battle
against Sweden, during which Onela is killed.

NOTE: Again, notice the way the poet moves from
the past to the present. You learn that two major
events occurred during Beowulf's reign as king—the
Frisian War and the Geats' feud with Sweden. It's
natural, now that Beowulf is an old man, for his memories of the past to play such a large role in the story,
that the memories, in fact, *are* the story. We know that
Beowulf will defeat the dragon and die in the process.
It's how Beowulf views his entire life that's most
important in part two.

The thief who stole the dragon's cup leads Beowulf
and his men to the dragon's castle. As Beowulf rests
on the shore outside the castle, he has a premonition
of his own death. He realizes that he's not as strong as
he was when he fought Grendel; the risk of dying is
more than a vague possibility. The poet takes this

opportunity to allow Beowulf to review his life. We learn how Hrethel took him from his father when Beowulf was seven and treated him like a son, reviving the theme of kinship, and the search for the lost father that recurs throughout the poem.

Hrethel, we are told, has three sons of his own—Herbald, Hathcyn, and Higlac. Beowulf recounts the story of how Hathcyn killed Herbald in a hunting accident, and of Hrethel's sadness at the loss of his son. Old age, as depicted in the poem, seems to be a time of great unhappiness, when all the success and pleasures of a long life are undermined by the loss of strength and power. Hrethel is powerless to avenge his son's death: a problem within one's own family is different from a feud between countries. Consequently, he can do nothing to relieve his grief.

Beowulf's meditation on his life is one of the most moving sections of the poem. Though old age has robbed him of his physical strength, his courage is truly heroic—he still thinks like a hero. His recitation is a study in contrasts between the sad and the joyous, as well as being a chronological history of what he considers his immediate family.

After Herbald dies, Hathcyn inherits the throne, only to die in yet another battle between the Geats and the Swedes. The tone of Beowulf's meditation changes once Higlac becomes king. As long as Beowulf was there to fight at his side, it was unnecessary for the Geat king to enlist help from other tribes. Beowulf's presence alone, so he tells us, was enough to ensure the success of the Geat nation. He sees himself as being "alone, and so it shall be forever." It's the hero's fate, as one whose courage is so much greater than anyone else's, to move through the world alone, to fight alone against the monsters, to stand alone at the front of every battle. His memories of his previous accomplishments give him the courage now, as an old warrior, to proceed with his endeavor against the dragon.

NOTE: Compare this speech with Beowulf's speeches preceding his battles against Grendel and Grendel's mother. Now that he's an old man has Beowulf's confidence in himself decreased?

Beowulf turns from his meditation on the past to address his fellow warriors. His accomplishments fill him with pride—but of a different sort than the negative pride Hrothgar warned him against earlier in the poem. He will fight against the dragon in the same way he fought against Grendel. As a hero it's his job to accomplish the impossible; as an old man he still wants one last moment of glory.

It's Beowulf who initiates the battle, waking the dragon with "a call so loud and clear that it reached through/The hoary rock, hung in the dragon's ear" (2552–54). During the first confrontation the dragon's flames melt Beowulf's shield. The aged warrior realizes now that fate is against him, but it doesn't prevent him from striking out against the dragon with his sword.

Beowulf manages to wound the dragon, but not fatally. The dragon responds by engulfing Beowulf with his fiery breath. Now that Beowulf appears to be losing the battle doesn't it seem to you that his comrades would come to his assistance? But the bonds of loyalty and kinship have broken down, a foreshadowing of the chaos that will befall the Geats after Beowulf dies. His fellow warriors flee, thinking only of saving their own lives. Individual survival has become more important than the code of honor and bravery—the bond of *comitatus*—that held society together. The response of the warriors to Beowulf's plight indicates that the values of this world are changing rapidly. Without the bond of *comitatus*, without a great leader to guide them, the state will surely fall apart.

VERSES 36–37

One of Beowulf's followers remains true to the bonds of kinship and loyalty. Wiglaf may not be cut from the same heroic mold as Beowulf, but he possesses the same energy and vigor that characterized Beowulf as a young warrior. (Parallel relations abound throughout the poem. Notice, for example, how the aging Beowulf resembles Hrothgar at the start of the poem.)

Read Wiglaf's speech to his comrades in light of what you've already learned about the warriors' code of ethics. As early as the Prologue, the poet informed us that it was a king's generosity toward his warriors that established the bonds of loyalty. In return for their loyalty he provided them with swords and armor, and shared with them the spoils of war.

Wiglaf realizes that for Beowulf it's a point of honor to fight the dragon alone. But he also realizes that for Beowulf "those days are over and gone/And now our lord must lean on younger/Arms" (*2646–48*). He tries to encourage his frightened comrades to come to Beowulf's assistance; he berates them, and mocks their manhood. But to no avail. The poet gives us a brief history of Wiglaf's sword.

NOTE: How do you interpret this? Some readers feel that the image of the sword as it's used throughout the poem is a symbol of the never-ending feuds between countries. People die in battle, but their swords survive and are used, in future battles, by their next of kin. Objects, the poet is telling us here, often have a longer history than people. Recall how after Beowulf killed Grendel's mother he gave Hrothgar the handle of the magic sword, and how Hrothgar read "the story of ancient wars between good and evil" in the runes on its shiny handle.)

Wiglaf rushes fearlessly into the thick of the battle, crying words of encouragement to Beowulf. The dragon hears him, and engulfs both the warriors with his flames. Beowulf attempts to crush the dragon's head with his old sword, Nagling, but the sword fails him and breaks into pieces. The monster charges again and thrusts its tusks into Beowulf's neck.

NOTE: Beowulf doesn't reject Wiglaf's assistance at this moment. It's more important to slay the dragon and protect his people than to preserve his legend as a warrior who fights alone. It's only as an old man that he realizes the advantage of working in collaboration with other people, and that the pride of the solitary hero only adds to the chaos of the world.

Wiglaf cleverly manages to wound the dragon with his sword, and Beowulf finishes the job by cutting the beast in half. "What they did," the poet tells us, "all men must do/When the time comes!" (2708–2709). Beowulf realizes that the wound in his neck is serious, and he prepares to die. In his speech to Wiglaf he bemoans the fact that he has no son to whom he can leave his armor. (Remember that the poem is filled with substitute sons and fathers. Wiglaf, then, as he bathes Beowulf's wounds, can be seen as the son Beowulf never had.)

Beowulf reviews his life. He sees his past in terms of all the things he never did: he swore no unholy oaths, began no wars without good reason, didn't shed the blood of any members of his family. His sin, if any, was his desire for wealth and fame. He wasn't content, the poet implies, with his God-given gifts, but craved the rewards that he felt were due him for his accomplishments.

VERSE 38

So gold can easily
Triumph, defeat the strongest of men,
No matter how deep it is hidden!

(2764–66)

How insignificant the dragon's treasure-hoard seems in comparison to the acts of bravery and honor that Beowulf accomplished during his life! Yet, as he dies, his main concern is to see the treasure that the dragon was guarding. The conflict between spiritual and material values is never more evident than in his last speech, where he thanks God for "this gold, these jewels." It's as if as an old man he's reverted to the pagan belief in objects, forgetting that it was with God's strength that he was able to be successful against his many adversaries.

"I sold my life/For this treasure," Beowulf tells Wiglaf, "and I sold it well" *(2798–99)*. The treasure-hoard, as described by the poet, is in a state of chaos—"piles of gleaming gold, precious gems, scattered on the floor"—much like the world itself. After all the feuds and all the endless battles, the dragon's treasure seems like a small reward.

Beowulf's last request is to have a tomb built in his honor. Like Hrothgar, he wants to create some kind of permanent monument to his successes—though permanence, as we've seen, is only an illusion. He gives his necklace, helmet, rings, and mailshirt to Wiglaf. It's the end of an era of prosperity and stability and the beginning of an age of chaos and disintegration. What hope does the world have without the bond between king and warrior?

VERSE 39

The cowardly Geat warriors emerge from the woods where they've been hiding and discover Wiglaf trying to revive the body of his king. Wiglaf's anger when he addresses them is undercut by the grief he feels over Beowulf's death. His speech is an elegy for the entire Geat tribe.

Once again the poet emphasizes the bond between warrior and king as essential to the stability of medieval society. Beowulf gave his followers the best weapons he could find, but when the time came to use them they "ran like cowards."

Wiglaf, with the true modesty of a devoted warrior, minimizes his role in killing the dragon. Do you think he does this to make his comrades feel guilty? Or is he trying to perpetuate Beowulf's status as a great hero?

He ends his speech by predicting that the Geats will forever be known as cowards, and that death would be preferable to a life "branded with disgrace."

VERSES 40–41

Wiglaf sends a messenger to the troop of Geat soldiers who are awaiting word on the outcome of the battle. In his address the nameless messenger continues Wiglaf's prediction that the Geats will now become targets of all their old enemies, most especially the Franks and the Swedes.

The messenger reviews the history of the feuds between the tribes. We hear, briefly, about the "bitter quarrel" that Higlac began with the Franks, during which the Geat king was killed. And in the poem's final—and possibly most violent—historical digression, the messenger recounts the long history of the feud between the Geats and the Swedes.

NOTE: These stories, which concern the death of kings (Higlac on one hand, and the Swedish king Ongentho on the other), should be seen in contrast with the story of Beowulf's own death. The story of the battle between the Geats and the Swedes includes many of the major themes that the poet has presented up to this point.

The old Swedish king Ongentho is depicted in combat with the young Geat warriors, Efor and Wulf. (Efor and Wulf collaborate on killing the king, in much the same way Beowulf and Wiglaf joined forces to destroy the dragon.) In keeping with the code between king and warrior, Efor and Wulf are rewarded by Higlac with great treasures. Killing, the poet is saying, is an acceptable act: it is the only way for the warriors to accumulate wealth and fame. Neither Efor nor Wulf is a particularly impressive warrior and neither of them seems to have any moral feelings about killing. They are motivated solely by the promise of rewards.

The messenger predicts that all the old feuds will begin again once the Geats' enemies learn that Beowulf is dead. It's time to bury the great hero—and with him, all the treasures that the dragon guarded for so long. Some readers feel that the messenger is really speaking in the voice of the poet himself, and that the poem's ultimate message is a condemnation of all the material objects that were so important to the kings, the warriors, and to medieval society in general. The messenger advises Beowulf's followers to melt the dragon's treasure-hoard in the same fire that consumes the hero's ashes: "Give it all of this golden pile,/ This terrible, uncounted heap of cups/And rings, bought with his blood" (3012–14). The age of laughter and prosperity is over. If the treasures aren't buried alongside Beowulf's ashes, they will surely fall into the hands of the Geats' enemies.

The messenger ends his speech by evoking the beasts of war: the raven, the eagle, and the wolf. You can almost feel the shadows darkening and the air growing still, an ominous silence broken only by the cries of these animals. As men plunder the treasures of their enemies, so these beasts, the poet reminds us, feed on the bodies of the dead warriors.

The Geats go to the scene of the battle and view the two dead bodies: Beowulf and the dragon. Yet the poet's main interest is the treasure-hoard, and once again he depicts the meaninglessness of all these objects for which people died and whole tribes were destroyed. The dragon guarded the treasure, killed men, and was killed in return. Is it all worth it?

VERSE 42

Hiding the treasure, the poet tells us, was a sign of man's greed. It went against the law of God. Eventually it led to Beowulf's death. The men who hid the treasure had cast a spell on it that was meant to last until the day of judgment. It was Beowulf's ill-fortune—and his fate—to fight the dragon and inherit his jewels.

NOTE: No one knows when one is going to die. A thief steals a cup from a dragon, and this seemingly trivial act leads to Beowulf's downfall. His death makes us wonder whether all his acts of courage were motivated by greed, as much as by a desire for fame and glory. In his dying moments the dragon's treasure seems to be his main concern. To give Beowulf the benefit of the doubt, we should view him as an essentially honorable person—a man who wanted to perform good deeds—who was unable to resolve the conflict between pagan and Christian values that dominated his lifetime.

In Wiglaf's final speech, the poet attempts to sum up the events that led to Beowulf's death. We learn that Beowulf's followers tried to prevent him from fighting the dragon, but that "fate, and his will, were too strong." Beowulf's life was worth more than all the treasures he earned by his acts of courage. Unlike Efor and Wulf and most of the other warriors, Beowulf's life had a moral value that set him apart from other men.

Wiglaf orders the lumber for Beowulf's funeral pyre. With seven other Geat warriors he enters the dragon's cave and gathers the treasure-hoard. Then, after rolling the dragon's body into the ocean, they load the treasures onto a wagon and bring them to the pyre.

VERSE 43

The Geats carry out Beowulf's final wishes. They build a huge funeral pyre, surrounding it with helmets, shields, and mailshirts. It's a time of great sadness and mourning. An old woman leads the mourners in "a song of misery," predicting the decline of the Geat nation. The smoke from the funeral pyre rises toward heaven with the words of her song—a final link, some readers feel, between the spiritual and earthly forces that dominate the world.

The Geats are aware that with Beowulf's death their lives have changed for the worse; there's no one to replace him. They build a tower on the sand, a monument containing the hero's ashes and all the dragon's treasures. Though Beowulf had hoped that his people would profit from the dragon's hoard, all the gold and jewels are useless, buried in the earth forever. It's the poem's great irony that all the material rewards that one earns during one's life can never be enough to stem the tide of fate. Everything in life is uncertain, even for a hero.

A STEP BEYOND

Tests and Answers
TESTS

Test 1

1. *Beowulf* may have been first told by a *scop*   _____
   who was a(n)
   A. traveling entertainer
   B. monk
   C. epic hero

2. Two conflicting codes in this poem are   _____
   A. Christian and pagan
   B. materialist and idealist
   C. political and spiritual

3. Beowulf sails to Denmark because   _____
   A. he wants to fight Grendel
   B. Hrothgar invited him
   C. a big reward was offered

4. Grendel is a descendant of   _____
   A. Satan
   B. Chaos
   C. Cain

5. Hrothgar once fought with   _____
   A. King Higlac
   B. Beowulf's father Edgetho
   C. The king of the Wulfings

6. The Finnsburg Episode is told to bring up   ____
   the theme of:
       I. treachery
      II. kinship
     III. revenge
   A. I and III only
   B. I and II only
   C. I, II, and III

7. Beowulf kills Grendel's mother with   ____
   A. a shaft of holy light
   B. her own son's claw
   C. a magical sword

8. Unlike Hrothgar, in his old age Beowulf   ____
   seeks
   A. a son figure
   B. one last moment of glory
   C. wisdom

9. The dragon begins to attack the Geats   ____
   because
   A. a cup was stolen from its hoard
   B. its son was killed
   C. God makes him punish the faithless
      Geats

10. After Beowulf dies, we sense that the Geats   ____
    will
    A. use the treasure wisely
    B. become prey to their enemies
    C. live in peace at last

11. One of the major themes of Beowulf is the contrast
    between youth and age. Discuss.

12. Analyze the various aspects of Beowulf's personality. In what ways do you think he's a hero?

13. Analyze the structure of the poem. Focus on how the historical digressions fit into the main narrative.

14. Define the following terms: *kenning, alliteration, litote*.

15. Why is the code of ethics between warrior and king so important to Anglo-Saxon society?

Test 2

1. This poem relates the adventures of the _____
   A. Anglos and the Saxons
   B. Celts and the Norsemen
   C. Danes and the Geats

2. Herot is the home built by _____
   A. Grendel
   B. Hrothgar
   C. Beowulf

3. Hrothgar is to young Beowulf as old Beowulf is to _____
   A. Unferth
   B. Wiglaf
   C. Brecca

4. *Comitatus* is _____
   A. the bond between king and warrior
   B. Christian charity
   C. courage in battle

5. When we first meet Beowulf, he appears _____
   A. calm and self-confident
   B. shy and uncertain
   C. boastful and rude

6. When Beowulf grabs Grendel's hand, the monster _____
   A. immediately wants to escape
   B. breathes fire on the roof
   C. calls for his mother

7. The *Beowulf* poet repeats scenes for the following reasons: _____
   I. for variety
   II. for emphasis
   III. as part of a courtly tradition
   A. I only
   B. III only
   C. I and II only

8. Grendel's mother kills   _____
    A. Hrothgar's friend Esher
    B. Beowulf's son
    C. Unferth

9. Hrothgar warns Beowulf against   _____
    A. greed
    B. pride
    C. too much trust in God

10. Beowulf becomes king of the Geats   _____
    A. when Higlac dies
    B. after Herdred, Higlac's son
    C. because he has killed the dragon

11. What do you learn about Anglo-Saxon society from reading the poem?

12. Define an epic. Discuss the reasons why you would describe *Beowulf* as an epic poem.

13. In what way was the poet influenced by Christian tradition? Explain.

14. Some critics feel that the major theme of the poem is the struggle between good and evil. Tell why you agree or disagree.

15. How does the society of the Danes and the Geats change in the course of the poem?

ANSWERS

Test 1

1. A   **2.** A   **3.** A   **4.** C   **5.** B   **6.** A

7. C   **8.** B   **9.** A   **10.** B

11. Compare the relationship between Beowulf as a young man and Hrothgar as an older king. See how this parallels the later relationship between Beowulf and Wiglaf. Note the characteristics of Beowulf's youthfulness by citing examples from his first speeches when he arrives in Denmark. Compare the tone and content of these speeches with Beowulf's speeches as an old man.

12. Note Beowulf's superhuman qualities (for instance, his ability to stay underwater for long periods of time, as he does during the battle with Grendel's mother) that set him apart from other men. Discuss how he treats other people, citing examples from the poem: his conversation with the Danish soldier when the Geats first arrive in Denmark, his dialogues with King Hrothgar and King Higlac. Discuss his personality in terms of his capacity for loyalty, forgiveness, and generosity. Does his desire for fame and glory make him less a hero? Talk about why you think he insists on fighting the dragon alone, and relate this idea to the idea of the hero as a solitary and tragic figure.

13. The poem is divided into two parts. In part one we see Beowulf as a young man, in part two as an aging king. The main narrative involves three battles: Beowulf and Grendel, Beowulf and Grendel's mother, Beowulf and the dragon. The poem can be described structurally by comparing parts one and two or by comparing the three battles. The poem can also be viewed as being structured around the character of Beowulf.

In the course of telling the main story the poet frequently digresses with a related story from the past. The relation of the historical digressions to the main narrative is another possible interpretation of how the poem was put together. Take any of the digressions—the Finnsburg Episode, for instance—and see how it relates to what's going on in the main narrative. Discuss how the stories from the past are meant to parallel and illuminate what's happening in the present.

14. A *kenning* is a phrase signifying a characteristic of a person or thing that the poet uses instead of naming that person or thing directly. For example: a warrior might be described as "the helmet-bearing one" or a king as a "ring-giver." *Alliteration* is the repetition of the same sounds or syllables in two or more words in a line. *Litotes* are a form of understatement, often intended to create a sense of irony. An example of litotes can be found in the poet's description of Beowulf after he returns to Geatland from Denmark (*2165–69*).

15. Throughout the poem (beginning with the description of Shild in the Prologue) we see how the code of *comitatus* forms the backbone of Anglo-Saxon society. The king known for his generosity will attract the most warriors. In return, the warrior will pledge his loyalty to the king and his country. Cite the Geat warriors' refusal (with the exception of Wiglaf) to help Beowulf when he fights the dragon. Refer to Wiglaf's speech to his cowardly comrades, and discuss the idea that, as Wiglaf puts it, death is better than the violation of the code.

Test 2

1. C   2. B   3. B   4. A   5. A   6. A

7. C   8. A   9. B   10. B

11. The poem deals with only one aspect of Anglo-Saxon society: the kings and the warriors. The thief who steals the cup from the dragon is perhaps the only character in the poem who isn't a member of the aristocracy. The life of the kings and the warriors is very formal and ritualistic. Their main forms of relaxation tend to be simple ones, like eating and drinking. Discuss women's role in the society and mention the women characters whom you think are most important.

12. *Beowulf* fits into the epic tradition that began with Homer's *The Iliad* and *The Odyssey* and Virgil's *The Aeneid*. Like these earlier poems, *Beowulf* deals with a few heroic events in the life of a single individual. Through an examination of this person's life the epic poet attempts to reflect the history of his time. (It would be a good idea to read the earlier epic poems and compare them to *Beowulf*.) Note the dignity of the style and tone, and the way past events are woven into the main narrative. Analyze Beowulf's relation to Hrothgar and Higlac, his feelings about the feud between the Danes and the Hathobards, and how his personality embodies the most important characteristics and conflicts of Anglo-Saxon society.

13. The poet was indebted to the Christian tradition as it existed in England at the end of the seventh century. His point of view, his references to the Bible, his ethical standards are all Christian; he's attempting to blend the pagan concept of fate with the Christian idea of grace. Beowulf defeats Unferth not by force, but by example, and Unferth hands over his sword, symbol of his strength. The audience for whom the poet was writing was obviously familiar with

the Christian references. At the approximate time that the poem was composed, most of the Anglo-Saxon world had converted to Christianity. It might be said that *Beowulf* was a pagan epic adapted to the feelings of a Christian world.

14. The monsters are necessary to the poem so that Beowulf can prove his heroic qualities. Beowulf is described as "the strongest man in the world" and in order to prove himself as a hero he has to fight against something superhuman. Although the monsters possess evil qualities that doesn't mean that Beowulf and the warriors are necessarily good. Analyze the characteristics of pagan society: the feuds, the conspiracies, the emphasis on material goods, the endless wars between countries. It's a society where killing is accepted and rewarded. In the poet's mind, society was as much a threat to itself as the monsters were.

15. The poem begins on a positive note: it's the beginning of a new reign of prosperity for the Danish people. The bond between king and warrior—*comitatus*—has never been stronger. A heroic figure like Beowulf is an accepted figure in this world. The way to win glory and fame is by risking your life and performing acts of extreme bravery and courage. By the end of the poem we see how the value of the bond between warrior and king has diminished in importance. Beowulf strives to perform one last heroic act—killing the dragon—and loses his life. The Geat dynasty is on the brink of disaster. The Danes are about to enter a feud with the Hathobards. Christianity is replacing paganism as the basis for ethical conduct.

Term Paper Ideas

1. Discuss the idea of *comitatus* and why it was so important to Anglo-Saxon society.

2. What are the qualities that make a hero? Cite the qualities in Beowulf's personality that you think are truly heroic?

3. Some readers describe Beowulf as being more like a god than a man. What are the qualities that make him human?

4. Compare Beowulf to Odysseus in Homer's *Odyssey* and Aeneas in Virgil's *Aeneid*.

5. How are the historical digressions important to the structure of the poem?

6. What is the relevance of the character Unferth to the poem?

7. Are Hrothgar's tears on Beowulf's departure from Denmark a sign of strength or weakness?

8. Compare Beowulf as a young warrior to Wiglaf.

9. Show how the influence of Christianity affected the lives of Beowulf, Hrothgar, and Anglo-Saxon society in general.

10. What is the role of women in Anglo-Saxon society? Are there any major women characters in the poem?

11. Why do you think the poet repeats the story of the battle between Beowulf and Grendel so frequently? Do these repetitions add to or subtract from the overall drama of the poem?

12. Analyze Hrothgar's sermon to Beowulf on the evils of pride. Discuss the ideas contained within this speech.

13. Why does Wiglaf predict that the Geat dynasty will collapse after Beowulf's death?

14. Compare "The Lay of the Last Survivor" to Hrothgar's sermon on pride.

15. Is Hrothgar himself guilty of excessive pride by building Herot? Discuss this in relation to the feeling of instability and transience that pervaded Anglo-Saxon life.

16. Discuss the father-son relationship between Hrothgar and Beowulf.

17. Define paganism. Discuss how paganism affected Beowulf's character, and what conflicts it created for the hero.

18. What makes *Beowulf* a great poem? Discuss the way the poet uses language—the precision with which he describes things, his narrative techniques.

19. Discuss the concept of revenge as it occurs throughout the poem. Do you think that revenge is part of the pagan or the Christian tradition?

20. Why does Beowulf insist on fighting the monster alone? Discuss this point in terms of what we know about the nature of the hero.

21. What is the poet's point of view? Does it remain the same throughout the poem or does it change from character to character?

22. Choose one of the historical digressions and show how it connects to the main narrative.

23. Discuss the image of "feasting" as it appears throughout the poem.

24. What does the violence of the battle scenes tell us about Anglo-Saxon society? Relate the notion of violence to the conflict between paganism and Christianity.

25. Who are the major characters in the poem other than Beowulf? Explain.

Further Reading

CRITICAL WORKS

Bloomfield, Joan. "The Style and Structure of *Beowulf*." *Review of English Studies*, XIV (1938): 396–403.

Brodeur, Arthur G. *The Art of Beowulf*. Berkeley: University of California Press, 1959.

Chambers, R. W. *Beowulf: An Introduction to the Study of the Poem*. Cambridge: Cambridge University Press, 1959.

Fry, Donald K. "The Artistry of *Beowulf*," from *The Beowulf Poet: A Collection of Critical Essays*, ed. Donald K. Fry. Englewood Cliffs, N.J.: Prentice-Hall, 1968.

Girvan, Ritchie. *Beowulf and the Seventh Century*. London: Methuen, 1935.

Irving, Edward B., Jr. *Introduction to Beowulf*. Englewood Cliffs, N.J.: Prentice-Hall, 1969.

Kennedy, Charles W. *Beowulf, The Oldest English Epic*. New York: Oxford University Press, 1964.

Lawrence, W. W. *Beowulf and Epic Tradition*. Cambridge, Mass.: Harvard University Press, 1928.

Nicholson, Lewis E., ed. *An Anthology of Beowulf Criticism*. Notre Dame, Ind.: University of Notre Dame Press, 1963. Includes the Tolkien article.

Rexroth, Kenneth. "Classics Revisited—IV: *Beowulf*," *Saturday Review*, April 10, 1965, p. 27.

Sisam, Kenneth. *The Structure of Beowulf*. London: Oxford University Press, 1965.

Tolkien, J. R. R. "*Beowulf*: The Monsters and the Critics," *Proceedings of the British Academy*, XXII (1936): 245–95.

ENGLISH TRANSLATIONS OF *BEOWULF*

Alexander, Michael. *Beowulf*. London: Penguin Books, 1973.

Kennedy, Charles W. *Beowulf*. New York: Oxford University Press, 1940.

Morgan, Edwin. *Beowulf*. Berkeley: University of California Press, 1964.

Raffel, Burton. *Beowulf*. New York: New American Library, 1963.

Glossary of Names

The spelling of names in this study guide are based on the Burton Raffel translation. Alternative spellings are given below in parentheses and italics.

Beo A Danish king. Son of Shild, father of Healfdane.

Beowulf Son of Edgetho, nephew of Higlac. King of the Geats. Born in A.D. 495, went to Denmark to battle Grendel in 515, became king of the Geats in 533.

Bonstan *(Beanstan)* Father of Brecca.

Brecca Chief of the Brondings. A young companion of Beowulf.

Brondings A Scandinavian tribe.

Brosing A possible reference to the Brisings, who made a necklace for the goddess Freyja.

Dagref *(Daeghrefn)* A Frank warrior, killed by Beowulf.

Eclaf *(Ecglaf)* Unferth's father.

Edgetho *(Ecgtheow)* Father of Beowulf, married to Hrethel's daughter.

Efor *(Eofor)* A Geat warrior. Kills Ongentho, and is given Higlac's daughter as a reward.

Emer *(Eomer)* Son of Offa.

Ermlaf *(Yrmenlaf)* A Danish nobleman, brother of Esher.

Ermric *(Eormenric)* King of the East Goths.

Esher *(Aeschere)* A Danish nobleman, one of Hrothgar's trusted friends. Killed by Grendel's mother.

Finn A Frisian king; husband of Hnaf's sister, Hildeburh.

Fitla *(Fitela)* Son of Siegmund.

Franks A West German tribe, located near the Rhine and Meuse rivers.

Freaw *(Freawaru)*   Hrothgar's daughter. She's given in marriage to Ingeld, in the hope of settling the quarrel between the Danes and the Hathobards.

Frisians   A West German people.

Froda   King of the Hathobards, father of Ingeld.

Garmund   Offa's father.

Geats   A tribe from southern Sweden. The exact identification and origin of this people is unknown.

Goths   A tribe originating in Poland. Settled near the Danube River in the third century A.D. Were wiped out by the Lombards at the end of the sixth century.

Grendel   A monster (descended from Cain) who lives at the bottom of a lake with his mother. Terrorizes the Danes until he's killed by Beowulf.

Halga   Son of Healfdane, brother of Hrothgar, father of Hrothulf.

Hama   A character in the series of tales about Ermric.

Hareth *(Haereth)*   Father of Higd.

Hathcyn *(Haethcyn)*   Son of Hrethel. He becomes king of the Geats after accidentally killing his brother, Herbald. Killed by Ongentho.

Hathlaf *(Heatholaf)*   A member of the Wulfing tribe, killed by Edgetho.

Hathobards   A German tribe, who may have lived on the south Baltic coast.

Healfdane *(Healfdene)*   A Danish king. Son of Beo, father of Hergar, Hrothgar, Halga, and Urs.

Hemming   A friend of Offa.

Hengest   A Danish warrior. Avenges the death of his leader, Hnaf, against the Finns.

Herbald *(Herebald)*   A prince of the Geats, Hrethel's son. Killed accidentally by his brother, Hathcyn.

Herdred *(Heardred)*   A king of the Geats, son of Higlac. He is killed by Onela, the Swedish king.

Hergar *(Heorogar)*   A Danish king, son of Healfdane.

Hermod *(Heremod)*   A Danish king whose bad character undermined his great military prowess.

Herot *(Heorot)*   Battle hall built by Hrothgar to celebrate his successes.

Herward *(Heoroweard)*   Hergar's son.

Higd *(Hygd)*   Wife of Higlac, daughter of Hareth.

Higlac *(Hygelac)*   A king of the Geats. Uncle of Beowulf, son of Hrethel, brother of Herbald and Hathcyn.

Hnaf *(Hnaef)*   A Danish king, killed by Finn.

Hondshew *(Hondscio)*   A Geat warrior. Accompanies Beowulf to Denmark and is killed by Grendel.

Hrethel   A king of the Geats. Higlac's father.

Hrethric   Son of Hrothgar.

Hrothgar   A Danish king. Son of Healfdane. While king his country is afflicted by the attacks of Grendel and Grendel's mother.

Hrothmund   Son of Hrothgar.

Hrothulf   Son of Halga. Though it's not mentioned in the poem, Hrothulf was to seize the Danish throne after Hrothgar's death, killing Hrethric, the legal heir.

Hrunting   Unferth's sword.

Ingeld   A prince of the Hathobards. Married to Freaw.

Jutes   A Frisian tribe.

Nagling   Beowulf's sword.

Offa   King of the Angles, husband of Thrith.

Onela   A Swedish king, son of Ongentho. Killed the Geat king Herdred and is later killed by his nephew.

Ongentho *(Ongentheow)*   A Swedish king. Killer of Hathcyn. Eventually killed by a group of Geats, led by Higlac.

Rennsburg   Location of the battle between the Swedes and Geats.

Shild *(Scyld)*   A Danish king.

Siegmund *(Sigemund)*   Legendary Germanic hero, whose story is recounted in the poem. Son of Vels, father of Fitla.

Swerting   Grandfather of Higlac.

Thrith *(Thryth)*   Offa's wife. A haughty and violent woman who is later tamed by her husband.

Unferth   A Danish warrior. Attempts to slander Beowulf's reputation when the hero arrives in Denmark.

Vels   Siegmund's father.

Wayland   A master smith celebrated in many Germanic poems.

Welthow *(Wealththeow)*   Wife of Hrothgar.

Wexstan *(Weoxstan)*   Wiglaf's father. Killed Onela's nephew, when the Swedish king invaded Geatland.

Wiglaf   A Geat warrior, who joined Beowulf in the fight against the dragon.

Wulf   A Geat warrior, brother of Efor.

Wulfgar   A Danish warrior. He informs Hrothgar of Beowulf's arrival in Denmark.

Wulfings *(Wylfings)*   A Germanic tribe who resided on the Baltic Sea.

Yrs   Daughter of Healfdane.

The Critics

Beowulf is essentially a balance, an opposition of ends
and beginnings. In its simplest terms it is a contrasted
description of two moments in a great life, rising and
setting; an elaboration of the ancient and intensely
moving contrast between youth and age, first achievement and final death.

> J. R. R. Tolkien, "Beowulf: The Mon-
> sters and the Critics," 1936

We have in *Beowulf* a story of giant-killing and
dragon-slaying. Why should we construct a legend of
the gods or a nature-myth to account for these tales?
Why must Grendel or his mother represent the tem-
pest, or the malaria, or the drear long winter nights?
We know that tales of giant-killers and dragon-slayers
have been current among the people of Europe for
thousands of years. Is it not far more easy to regard the
story of the fight between Beowulf and Grendel merely
as a fairy tale, glorified into an epic?

> R. W. Chambers, *Beowulf: An Intro-
> duction to the Study of the Poem*, 1959

The poet's consistency of tone reveals his mastery of
texture and structure, mostly in the handling of digressions of various length. A long one, such as the Finnsburg episode, can set the grim past of the Danes into an
atmosphere of treachery in Hrothgar's court. The overwhelming tension of that long Frisian winter with its
resolution by slaughter is emblematic and prophetic of
the impending horrors of Hrothulf's revolt and the
Hathobard feud.

> Donald K. Fry, "The Artistry of Beo-
> wulf," 1968

The Christian influence in the *Beowulf* is a matter of
transforming spirit, rather than of reference to dogma
or doctrine. And it is, in the main, an influence reflect-
ing the Old Testament rather than the New. The poem
contains specific references to Cain's murder of Abel,
and to the stories of the Creation, the giants and the
Flood. But we find no such allusions to New Testament

themes. . . . Indeed, considering the nature of the material with which the poet is working, we should hardly expect such references.

Charles W. Kennedy, *Beowulf, The Oldest English Epic*, 1964

. . . in this work the poet was not much concerned with Christianity and paganism. Beowulf was a hero mainly because of his deeds. All his adventures come from pagan stories, and the pagan motives and actions persist. Hrothgar is made eminent by his speeches, which were not governed by pagan tradition. The Christian poet was free to mold them as he wished, and so to make belief in God a leading figure of the character. He was likely to make the most of it, since Hrothgar is not just the pathetic figure of a king incapable through old age of protecting his people: he is a famous hero, still great because of his wisdom and goodness.

Kenneth Sisam, *The Structure of Beowulf*, 1965

The most unexpected quality in *Beowulf* is its abiding communication of joy. In contrast with the Mediterranean glitter of the *Odyssey* . . . *Beowulf* takes place in an atmosphere of semi-darkness, the gloom of fire-lit halls, stormy wastelands, and underwater caverns. It is full of blood and fierceness. . . . Men exult in their conflict with each other and the elements. Even Grendel and his mother are serious in the way Greek demons never are. They may be horrors survived from the pagan Norse world of frost giants, wolf men, and dragons of the waters, but nobody would ever dream of calling them frivolous. They share Beowulf's dogged earnestness; what they lack is his joy. . . .

Kenneth Rexroth, "Classics Revisited—IV: Beowulf," 1965

Certain peculiarities in the structure of *Beowulf* can hardly fail to strike the reader. (1) The poem is not a biography of Beowulf, nor yet an episode in his life—it is 2 distinct episodes: The Grendel business and the dragon business, joined by a narrow bridge. (2) Both these stories are broken in upon by digressions: some of these concern Beowulf himself, so that we get a fairly complete idea of the life of our hero . . . (3) Even apart from these digressions, the narrative is often hampered: the poet begins his story, diverges and returns. (4) The traces of Christian thought and knowledge which meet us from time to time seem to belong to a different world from that of the Germanic life in which our poem has its roots.

R. W. Chambers: *Beowulf: An Introduction to the Study of the Poem*, 1959

NOTES

NOTES